THE STORY OF MARRIAGE

JOHN & LISA
BEVERE

The Story of Marriage
Copyright © 2014 by John P. Bevere, Jr. and Lisa Bevere

PUBLISHED BY: MESSENGER INTERNATIONAL
P.O. Box 888
Palmer Lake, CO 80133-0888
MessengerInternational.org

Unless otherwise indicated, all Scripture quotations are taken from the Holy Bible, New Living Translation, copyright © 1996, 2004, 2007, 2013 by Tyndale House Foundation. Used by permission of Tyndale House Publishers, Inc., Carol Stream, Illinois 60188. All rights reserved.

Scripture quotations marked NKJV taken from the New King James Version®. Copyright © 1982 by Thomas Nelson, Inc. Used by permission. All rights reserved. Scripture quotations marked AMP are taken from the AMPLIFIED® Bible. Copyright © 1954, 1958, 1962, 1964, 1965, 1987 by The Lockman Foundation. Used by permission. (www.Lockman.org) Scripture quotations marked ESV are from The Holy Bible, English Standard Version® (ESV®), copyright © 2001 by Crossway, a publishing ministry of Good News Publishers. Used by permission. All rights reserved. Scripture quotations marked GNT are from the Good News Translation in Today's English Version – Second Edition Copyright © 1992 by American Bible Society. Used by Permission. Scripture quotations marked GW taken from GOD'S WORD®. Copyright 1995 God's Word to the Nations. Used by permission of Baker Publishing Group. All rights reserved. Scripture quotations marked PHILLIPS are from J.B. Phillips, "The New Testament in Modern English," 1962 edition, published by HarperCollins. Scripture quotations marked The Message are taken from THE MESSAGE. Copyright © 1993, 1994, 1995, 1996, 2000, 2001, 2002. Used by permission of Tyndale House Publishers. Scripture quotations marked TLB are taken from The Living Bible copyright © 1971. Used by permission of Tyndale House Publishers, Inc., Carol Stream, Illinois 60188. All rights reserved. Scripture quotations marked NIV are taken from the HOLY BIBLE, NEW INTERNATIONAL VERSION ®. NIV®. Copyright © 1973, 1978, 1984, 2011 by Biblica, Inc.®. Used by permission. All rights reserved worldwide. Note: Some Scripture quotations marked NIV are taken from the HOLY BIBLE, NEW INTERNATIONAL VERSION ®. NIV®. Copyright © 1973, 1978, 1984 by Biblica, Inc.® Used by permission. All rights reserved worldwide. The "NIV" and "New International Version" trademarks are registered in the United States Patent and Trademark Office by International Bible Society. Use of either trademark requires the permission of International Bible Society.

Unless otherwise noted, bold treatment used in Scripture quotes and italics or bold treatment used in other quotes indicate the author's added emphasis.

ISBN: 978-1-933185-91-0
ISBN: 978-1-933185-93-4 (electronic)

SPECIAL SALES
Pastors, churches, and ministry leaders can receive special discounts when purchasing Messenger International resources. For information, please visit MessengerInternational.org or call 1-800-648-1477.

DISCUSSION QUESTIONS & DEVOTIONS WRITTEN & EDITED BY:
Vincent M. Newfield, New Fields & Company
P.O. Box 622
Hillsboro, Missouri 63050
www.newfieldscreativeservices.com

DESIGN SERVICES & PRINT PRODUCTION:
The Eastco Group
3646 California Rd.
Orchard Park, NY 14127
www.theeastcogroup.com

Cover artwork: Allan Nygren
Designer: Heather Huether

Printed in Canada

Acknowledgments

To our children, their spouses, and our grandchildren, in so many ways you are the reasons our story of marriage was written. We rejoice as we watch each of you rise and love one another so well.

Brave Addison, only eternity will measure your contribution accurately. To say we couldn't have done this without you falls far short of the truth. Thank you for persevering and merging our words with scriptural wisdom to create something that will touch lives.

Lovely, wise Jaylynn, your winsome attitude and excellent diligence have woven The Story of Marriage so well. May all that you've sown in this field overtake your life.

To Vincent and Allison, thank you for all you have done to help us create the devotions. Your work has enriched and enlarged this book.

To the team members and partners of Messenger International, thank you for standing with us. We couldn't have asked God for more loyal and true friends to journey with us in reaching out to the nations of the world with the glorious gospel of Jesus Christ.

Most of all, thank You, Father God, for Your unfailing love; and Jesus our King, for giving Your precious life; and You, Holy Spirit, for Your amazing power, comfort, teaching, and intimate fellowship. Thank You for never leaving or forsaking us.

CONTENTS

About This Interactive Book

This book may be read cover to cover, just like any other book. However, we encourage you to explore the optional interactive elements for a more personalized experience:

Each chapter of this book is divided into five suggested daily readings with corresponding devotions at the end of the chapter. You can choose to complete one reading and one devotion per day, or you can adapt these elements to your preference. We suggest that those participating in a group study complete the reading and devotions for one chapter per week.

If you are reading this book as part of the Messenger Series study on *The Story of Marriage*, we recommend that you watch or listen to each week's teaching session and answer the discussion questions as a group. Then, read the chapter in the book and complete the devotions. There is one teaching session for each chapter in this book. Discussion questions for each chapter are located after the daily devotions.

Enjoy!

Introduction

You may be asking, "Why another message about marriage?" This was our first reaction as well.

There are three reasons we wrote this book. First, we felt God leading us to. Next, our children and staff asked us to. And finally, many of you requested it as well.

We felt there was an abundance of excellent marriage resources on the market, many of which we have benefited from ourselves. Yet when we looked a bit closer, we noticed a gap. We discovered that a number of these resources were written predominantly from the viewpoint of one spouse or the other. A great marriage is the product of great partnership, so we believe there is value in our being able to share on this topic together.

We also know that every story is different—ours included. We are both, shall we say, *strong-willed* individuals. We have been married for more than three decades, and during that time, we have faced unique challenges. We realized that because our experiences were unique, our perspective would be as well.

Furthermore, we wanted to encourage men and women to see that marriage is not a mold that confines them. We believe everyone has the creative license to design their marriage as best suits their individual needs and divine purpose. We hope this book helps you discover and write your unique story.

Who This Book Is For

This book is for those preparing to marry, the already married, and anyone who wants to gain a better understanding of marriage.

Because we live in a day when there is so much divorce and distortion, many are afraid to even begin their stories. What you have seen need not define what lies before you.

Then there are those who feel trapped in the middle of a chapter they don't like. We don't want you to close the book on your marriage. We want to help you turn the page.

There are also countless friends who believed their love stories would never end, only to discover the pages had been abruptly torn from their lives by divorce or the loss of a spouse. Your story isn't over.

This is not a comprehensive book discussing every facet of marriage. Volumes could be written on the subject, and we don't have all the answers. Yet we decided to pen our story—including many of our most broken moments—because we know what we have lived and believe it will help others.

Finally, Jesus still thinks marriage is a story worth telling. It is His framework for how He loves us. We pray these pages stir faith, hope, and love in both the single and married, both the young and the well along in years. We dare you to dream again!

ONE

The Original Plan

The LORD God made all sorts of trees grow up from the ground—trees that were beautiful and that produced delicious fruit. In the middle of the garden he placed the tree of life and the tree of the knowledge of good and evil.

—Genesis 2:9

Day 1

Once upon a time, there was a garden wrapped around two trees. As you may already know, this was no ordinary garden. It existed free of struggle and decay. Rivers traversed Eden's landscape, supplying pure, crystalline water to all that inhabited the garden.

We can only imagine the magnificence of the trees that grew in such an environment. Each was a flawless symbol of life rooted in rich soil, awakened by cascading water, and nourished by radiant—yet tempered—sunshine. There were many trees in the garden, but Scripture only mentions two: the tree of life and the tree of the knowledge of good and evil. Both of these trees enjoyed the same immaculate and uncontaminated conditions—a state of existence that this fallen earth could never replicate. Yet one tree spawned life, the other death.

You have probably heard this tale before, for every story of marriage has its origin with these two trees of Eden. In so many ways, our marriages can be likened to trees of life. Marriages grow at different rates in different seasons and do best when anchored by mature roots. They experience both fruit-bearing and barren years, as well as years of exceptional growth and others when growth is stunted. Each marriage is affected by its native climate, varying seasons, and buffeting storms, yet marriage offers shelter from life's ever-changing winds.

The image on this book's cover provides a glimpse into the life of a tree. What we see in this collection of rings is actually the story of the tree's life—the fingerprint of its journey.

In school, many of us learned basic dendrology (the study of woody plants) and can roughly determine the age of a tree by counting its rings. While the two of us might be proficient at counting a tree's rings, we are far from being dendrologists (although we do love a good tree). In addition to a tree's exact age, experts of tree lore could provide us with intimate details of a tree's life simply by observing its cross section. To the trained eye, each ring is a story. The varying band widths tell if the tree experienced a mild or exceptionally harsh winter, revealing patterns of drought or abundant rain. A close inspection would reveal incidents of injury and attacks of pestilence. Each ring is a year of seasons, circular in fashion and unique in nature.

Each year of marriage could be likened to the path of a tree ring: circular in fashion and unique in nature. Anniversaries note the end of one year and the beginning of the next. The annual date is explicitly marked, but the months, weeks, and days that fill the calendar year are a collection of joy, pain, work, and even surprises.

Your Story

As you begin this journey with us, remember that your story (or future story) is just that: *it is yours.* Every life and marriage is a collection of joys, victories, and challenges. For too long, much of the Church has been content to offer generic prescriptions for the problems ailing our marriages. We've heard, "Wives, submit. Husbands, love." Although there is truth and value in this, frankly, there is no one-size-fits-all guide to building a marriage, because each marriage comes with its own unique fingerprint.

Let's look at it this way. The blueprints for every home include a foundation, supporting walls, and a roof, but the architect has the creative freedom to vary the design according to the specific needs and desires of its inhabitants. So it is with our marriages. We are granted the creative license to design them so they will be best suited to us. Each domain should look different and have the freedom to vary with the seasons of life. In our marriage, for example, we are moving into a time in which parenting will no longer be our dominant household role. This means it won't be long before our house will not need as many bedrooms as it has in the past. Such change in our marriages is as natural as the changing of seasons. All of this is normal.

There are universal, eternal truths and values that will propel your marriage into everything God has called it to be. God wants each marriage to be built with love, respect, joy, submission, provision, faithfulness, nurture, intimacy, and legacy—to name a few. But the way these building blocks are expressed in your life will reflect the uniqueness of your personality and the season of your marriage. God outlines the major principles but leaves room for your expression in the particulars.

God loves diversity. One glance at creation will confirm this. We want to make it clear from the start that we do not believe all couples fit into a generic marriage mold. In our day, more often than not both spouses work outside the home (in 2012, nearly 60% of working age women in the United States were active in the labor force[1]), and a wife might earn more than her husband. Her ability to produce income does not mean that she is not submissive or that he is not a leader. It simply means that both are contributing to the household income, which means their marriage most likely looks different than their grandparents' did.

Our marriage does. We both work and we are both leaders outside of our marriage. Sometimes we work together (as with this book), sometimes we work apart, but the goal of our marriage and our underlying values do not waver. The husband and wife relationship roles do not vary with our ability to produce income.

In that first garden, God told both Adam and Eve to be fruitful and multiply. He did not say that Eve was to stay home and manage Adam's multiplication. The virtuous woman of Proverbs 31 was an amazing household manager and entrepreneur. If that is what sounds right for your marriage, do it! Or one of you may want to stay home full-time—with children or without them. There is nothing wrong with either of these approaches.

At first it seems natural to assume that what has worked so well for others will work well for all. But we are in unique days with unique challenges on every front. We want your marriage strong. This means you must have the freedom to build the marriage of your dreams, not the marriage of someone else's dreams.

We encourage you to take a moment to ask God's Spirit, who is the Spirit of truth, to reveal how His eternal truths can transform your marriage into a specialized union—the one He designed just for you before the beginning of time.

Day 2

When Your Story Is Challenged

The number of years in a journey doesn't tell its full story. A marriage of fifty years might be fifty years of hardship or fifty years of perpetual bliss. But more often than not, marriage is a collage of varying and diverse seasons.

When we look at the image of the tree on this book's cover, it is evident that every ring increases the diameter of the tree. Regardless of whether a year was one of difficulty or abundance, it added breadth to the story and meaning to the journey. Would John Bunyan's *The Pilgrim's Progress*—a book that has been in print for over three centuries—be an enduring masterpiece if Christian (the story's main character) had arrived at the Celestial City (his destination) without experiencing the Slough of Despond or triumphing over the giant Despair? Without the complex weaving of joys and challenges, his story would be boring and uneventful. The perils Christian endures and overcomes are what make his story worth reading. The challenges in our marriages have the potential to infuse our stories with similar excitement and meaning.

Don't despise moments of discouragement. Use them to draw on the grace of God and discover His divine strength that will defy the limits of your emotional and spiritual capacity. Over the course of more than three decades of marriage, we've discovered that the very moments that seemed to be the darkest later became beacons to light our way. They compelled us to rise up and take a stand. Your current struggles can become some of the greatest moments in your story.

The Spirit of Marriage

Before we dive into the story of marriage, let's take a moment to explore its purpose. There is no doubt that marriage is wonderful, but at times it is a painful process. Most of us tend to have a lot more patience with the pain of a process if we understand its purpose. For instance, you can endure a couple of hours in a dentist's chair if you know the procedure will accomplish the purpose of eradicating an incessant toothache. In your marriage, you have probably experienced days that feel more like time in a dentist's chair than a stroll on a beach (and if you haven't yet, you will). It's in those painful moments that an awareness of your purpose is most vital.

Today the purpose of marriage is in question, and because many people don't understand the purpose of their unions, they are quick to jump ship when turbulent waters rock their boats. Others argue that the entire institution of marriage is more broken than whole and it needs to be renegotiated or expunged. Some even suggest that marriage contracts should be limited to a predetermined length of time—forever is too much to expect of any of us, it seems. These people argue that it is unrealistic to make decisions about how we're going to feel twenty years from now when we can hardly control how we're going to feel tomorrow.

In the well-known song "Ms. Jackson," hip-hop group OutKast expressed a popular sentiment:

Me and your daughter
Got a special thing going on
You say it's puppy love
We say it's full grown
Hope that we feel this, feel this way forever
You can plan a pretty picnic
But you can't predict the weather

"Ms. Jackson" is a man's apology to the mother of a young girl he impregnated but no longer feels love toward. Sadly, this song perfectly reflects a prevalent view of love and marriage: they're supposed to make *me* feel good. This perspective is based on the beliefs that our emotions tell us what is right and wrong and that we are incapable of managing them. If I don't feel happy, then obviously I have to make a change. After all, I can't control how I feel any more than I can control the changing of the seasons. Or as OutKast puts it, you can plan a pretty picnic but you can't predict the weather.

There are others who want the definition of marriage to adapt with the times. They ask, "Why can't we be more flexible? If this institution is going to survive, it needs to expand to include unions between a man and a man or a woman and a woman." Certain celebrities are even refusing to get married until the parameters of marriage have been renegotiated. (To be clear, each marriage should always be growing and adapting, but the definition and participants of marriage do not change.)

So to whom should we listen? Who has the right to define—or redefine—marriage? Who has the credentials to tell us how marriage should impact our lives?

We believe that God is the only One who holds this right. His Word declares:

> GOD, not you, made marriage. His Spirit inhabits even the smallest details of marriage. …So guard the spirit of marriage within you. (Malachi 2:15 The Message)

This verse leaves no room for doubt: "God, not you, made marriage." Not only did He create marriage, but He is also personally involved in the process of two people becoming one. Every marriage is made up of many different elements, some simple and some wildly complex, yet God quickens (or brings life to) marriage's most intimate details by His Spirit.

Notice that Malachi 2:15 says, "[God's] Spirit inhabits even the smallest details of marriage." In other words, God allows us creative expression in marriage, but He retains all Creator rights as to what it is and whom it includes. Marriage cannot be recreated without His consent and participation, and He is clear on foundational issues: "I am the LORD, and I do not change" (Malachi 3:6).

Back Again to Eden

Let's head back to the garden. Remember the two trees? One of them, the tree of the knowledge of good and evil, was the only tree whose fruit was forbidden to Adam and Eve. God warned that if they ate its fruit, they would die. But something about the tree caused them to turn a deaf ear to God's warning and partake of the forbidden fruit.

> When the woman saw that the fruit of the tree was good for food and pleasing to the eye, and also *desirable for gaining wisdom*...
> (Genesis 3:6 NIV, emphasis added)

Certainly many trees in this garden were good for food and pleasant to look at. But a tree whose fruit had the power to elevate one to the status of God was quite another thing. Eve thought there was something more than what she had already been given. We find it amazing that the woman would grasp at something she was not to have (equality with God) and in the process lose something she already had the potential to possess (wisdom).

Adam and Eve desired to be like God apart from His influence and authority. They grasped at a role that was not theirs to take. This stands in stark contrast to the choice made by one of their descendants:

> [Jesus], being in very nature God, did not consider equality with God something to be grasped... (Philippians 2:6 NIV)

Adam and Eve were made in the image of God, but not equal to Him. The *image* of something speaks of a reflection, not a representation in its entirety. The false promise of equality with God caused the man and woman to think they were receiving something, when in actuality they both lost. They did not receive wisdom; they accepted a deception.[2]

The deceived and disobedient couple was banished from the garden. They would never again have access to the fruit found on the tree of life. Without this living fruit, Adam and Eve were doomed to mortality. They died, and their garden is long gone. Yet in a way they live, because we are their offspring. Men and women no longer have individual immortality on this earth, but marriage is a way for life to continue through reproduction.

The good news is that the cross of Christ is now our ultimate tree of life. It restores everything that was lost in the garden. And a godly marriage can serve as a life-perpetuating tree. It provides the necessary framework for both legacy and intimacy. This is why it is so important to God that we honor marriage, guard its spirit, and love each other well.

It doesn't take a relationship guru to tell us something significant has been lost in translation between the garden and now. Many marriages are the opposite of a life-perpetuating tree. Divorce, adultery, disappointment, unhappiness, and offense ravage our marriages and homes. Because of these lapses in love, many do not understand the purpose of marriage—or why they'd even want to marry. Others who are married are just trying to survive the crossfire. To them, marriage isn't a safe haven. It's a war zone.

Day 3

The Source of Love

..."The Gentiles blaspheme the name of God because of you." (Romans 2:24)

When we, the Body of Christ, do not live and love well, people will blaspheme the name of God. This isn't surprising, for if we call ourselves "Christian," we claim to be ambassadors of Christ. The Apostle Paul wrote:

For God was in Christ, reconciling the world to himself, no longer counting people's sins against them. And he gave us this wonderful message of reconciliation. So we are Christ's ambassadors; God is making his appeal through us. We speak for Christ... (2 Corinthians 5:19-20)

An ambassador is an authorized messenger or representative.[3] As Christians, we speak for Christ. What a privilege! We have been invited, even charged, to participate in God's ministry of reconciliation. We speak for God with our words and actions. This is our purpose in life. We are co-laborers with God who advance His kingdom on the earth.

So what has Christ asked us, His ambassadors, to do? Jesus said, "So now I am giving you a new commandment: Love each other. Just as I have loved you, you should love each other" (John 13:34).

Thankfully this mission is not something we must accomplish through our own willpower. Scripture makes it clear that to fulfill our purpose, we must first be in Christ—heirs of His grace through His saving work on the cross. Only then can we operate in the transforming power of His Spirit, and only then can we love one another as He loves us.

Under the new covenant of grace, God never gives us a command that He will not empower us to fulfill. Because we are in Christ, His Spirit will enable our marriages and individual lives to reveal His presence and love to the world. However, we cannot reveal His love until we first experience it for ourselves. In Ephesians 3:16-19, Paul offers the key to receiving the power of Christ's love:

I pray that from his glorious, unlimited resources he will empower you with inner strength through his Spirit. Then Christ will make his home in your hearts as you trust in him. Your roots will grow down into God's love and keep you strong. And may you have the power to understand, as all God's people should, how wide, how long, how high, and how deep his love is. May you experience the love of Christ, though it is too great to understand fully. *Then* you will be made complete with all the fullness of life and power that comes from God. (emphasis added)

In order to receive the revelation of Christ's love, we first have to allow God to empower us with inner strength through His Spirit. But this cannot happen if you have not surrendered your life to Him. Once your life is His, you will have the opportunity to continually grow in His love, a journey that will ultimately lead to a full and whole life. (To learn more about surrendering your life to Christ, see page 243.)

Just two verses after Paul wrote about the power that comes from knowing Christ's love, he explained this power's purpose:

Therefore I...beg you to *lead a life worthy of your calling*, for you have been called by God. Always be humble and gentle. Be patient with each other, making allowance for each other's faults because of your love. Make every effort to keep yourselves united in the Spirit, binding yourselves together with peace. (Ephesians 4:1-3, emphasis added)

Notice Paul wrote, "lead a life worthy of your calling." Again, he is speaking of our purpose: to reveal God's love, truth, and way of life (His kingdom) to the world. None of this is possible without an experiential knowledge of God's love. Theoretical knowledge won't do. Only when we possess personal experience of God's love are we empowered to build lives—and marriages—worthy of our callings.

In this passage, Paul described certain behavioral patterns that sound a lot like marriage best practices: be humble, be gentle, be patient, make allowances for each other's faults, and make every effort to keep yourselves united in peace. It's no coincidence that in the very next chapter of Ephesians, we find some of the Bible's most famous verses on marriage. (Remember, chapter and verse designations were added by the church in the thirteenth century and did not appear in Paul's original letter.) Could it be that in Ephesians 1-4, Paul was preparing the hearts of his readers for what he was about to share—radical truths about marriage that would require radical knowledge of the love of God?

So here's the progression: Before you can love well (whether it be your spouse or anyone else), you must first discover the depths of God's love for you. Your knowledge of God's love cannot be based on second-hand information; you have to experience it for yourself. When you experience the love of Christ, "you will be made complete with all the fullness of life and power that comes from God." Only then can you lead a life worthy of your calling. The power for living and loving well comes from intimate knowledge of God's immense love for you.

The Purpose of Marriage

If your individual purpose is to be a representation of Christ on the earth, what is the purpose of your marriage?

Let's start with this: God is love. Love isn't just something God does. It's not just something He has. It's who He is. Marriage is an institution of love, the first institution God established. Not only is marriage the first institution established by God, it is also the poetic symbolism that He uses to represent the depths of His love for and commitment to us, His Church and bride. The bride and groom are a picture of the Church and Christ.

Because of this profound symbolism, there is an even deeper, darker intent behind the assault against marriage, a motive too few recognize. The attacks against marriage—its definition, designation, and divine roots—are about more than politics or social progress. Scripture makes it clear that we do not merely wrestle with flesh and blood, that our adversary is not a government or organization (see Ephesians 6:12). There is an ancient foe—the enemy of our souls—working behind the scenes to twist and pervert the divine merger. He will not stop attacking marriage until he has utterly distorted our frame of reference for the way God loves and relates to His people. The last thing Satan wants is for us to discover and receive God's transforming love. But by the grace of God, we can defeat our foe and embrace everything that God desires in and for our marriages.

What Does Jesus Think?

Not only did God make marriage; He also has a plan and purpose for it that hasn't changed. Although the debate about the particulars of marriage has been a hot topic for thousands of years, He still stands firmly behind His original plan. Look at what Jesus said to the Pharisees in one of His most famous conversations concerning marriage:

> One day the Pharisees were badgering him: "Is it legal for a man to divorce his wife for any reason?"
>
> He answered, "Haven't you read in your Bible that the Creator originally made man and woman for each other, male and female? And because of this, a man leaves father and mother and is firmly bonded to his wife, becoming one flesh—no longer two bodies but one. Because God created this organic union of the two sexes, no one should desecrate his art by cutting them apart." (Matthew 19:3-6 The Message)

The Pharisees were content to know what was legal, but Jesus wanted them to comprehend the power of love.

We can't deny the fact that God originally planned men and women for each other. In marriage, they leave their parents to form living unions. Once the two sexes are joined, no one should sever their merger.

Why Does God Care about Divorce?

The Message calls divorce a desecration of God's art. It's the fact that marriage is God's art—something He created—that makes divorce such a big deal.

To desecrate is to treat something sacred with violent disrespect.[4] Synonyms of desecrate include words like blaspheme, malign, defile, vandalize, insult, and violate. These extreme terms all convey a sense of violence. We have referenced The Message paraphrase, but every translation conveys the weightiness of dividing what God has united. And through proper contextual study, we can safely deduce that Jesus is speaking of all marriages.[5]

Can you imagine how the world would respond if someone desecrated Leonardo Da Vinci's *Mona Lisa*? Every news outlet would pick up the story. The perpetrator would be condemned by society and would probably spend the remainder of his or her life in prison. How could anyone dare to desecrate one of humanity's greatest works of art? Leonardo would roll over in his grave.

Well, God views marriage as one of the greatest works of art to be expressed through His favorite creation. His passion for marriage is evident in Jesus' response to the Pharisees. They found His words too great for them to handle, so they simply refused to answer Him. Unable to comprehend marriage in light of God's original intent, they hid behind the Law of Moses—an approach that gave them the license to leave rather than the empowerment to stay.

They shot back in rebuttal, "If that's so, why did Moses give instructions for divorce papers and divorce procedures?"

Jesus said, "Moses provided for divorce as a concession to your hard heartedness, but it is not part of God's original plan. I'm holding you to the original plan, and holding you liable for adultery if you divorce your faithful wife and then marry someone else. I make an exception in cases where the spouse has committed adultery." (Matthew 19:7-9 The Message)

Under the Law of Moses, concessions were made because of the hardness of the human heart. This was a provision, not God's original purpose. Make no mistake; God hates the effects of divorce. When a husband and wife are separated, one of the mysteries of God's creation (as marriage is described in Ephesians 5:31-32) is violated and torn apart.

Day 4

A New Heart

…"I'm holding you to the original plan, and holding you liable for adultery if you divorce your faithful wife and then marry someone else.…" (Matthew 19:9 The Message)

Again, Jesus will never ask us to do something that He will not enable us to accomplish. He holds us to God's original plan for marriage because He is willing to equip us to live it. The Law of Moses made allowances for the hardhearted, but through Jesus' sacrifice we receive new hearts born of the Spirit rather than of stone.

"…I will give you a new heart, and I will put a new spirit in you. I will take out your stony, stubborn heart and give you a tender, responsive heart." (Ezekiel 36:26)

We see this echoed in the New Testament. The Apostle Paul encouraged us with these words:

…We know how dearly God loves us, because he has given us the Holy Spirit to fill our hearts with his love. (Romans 5:5)

This newness of heart is not something we can muster. It's dependent on God's power and the might of His love. We are, however, responsible to humble ourselves and accept that power. Keep in mind that God will never force His love on you. He is a gentleman who never imposes Himself on us.

Because we have new hearts, ones capable of receiving Christ's love, we can now embrace Jesus' daunting statement on God's original plan for marriage and divorce.

The Message uses the word *liable* (meaning "responsible by law; legally answerable"[6]) to describe the state of someone who divorces a faithful spouse. We know this may sound like a tall order, but if God holds us to this standard, He is more than willing to give us the grace to fulfill it. But because the journey isn't easy or automatic, too many opt out exactly when they should press in.

According to one study, two out of three unhappily married couples will become happy with their marriages within five years, provided they don't divorce.[7] So don't give up! We don't know the state of your marriage at this moment, but even if you feel helpless, there is hope. Your breakthrough may be just around the corner. Jesus came to make good marriages better and broken marriages whole.*

The Exception

…"I make an exception in cases where the spouse has committed adultery." (Matthew 19:9 The Message)

Jesus made it clear that there is an exception to the original plan. Even in the case of adultery, however, ending a marriage is a matter of choice. If your spouse has been unfaithful, you don't have to stay, but you also don't have to leave. Whichever course you choose, you do have to forgive.

---

*You should never stay in a situation that is dangerous to you or your children. If there is abuse in your marriage, please take immediate action to stay safe. Contact your church or local authorities for further support and guidance.

There is a vast difference between forgiveness and reconciliation. You should forgive someone who robs from you, but that does not mean you have to invite the thief into your home. Reconciliation is only possible if a couple can be restored to a place of oneness after a grievous breach of covenant, faith, and trust.

We have never suffered the breach of adultery, but we have stood by friends who experienced its horrors. Some of these couples chose to embrace reconciliation. They did the hard work of repairing the broken pieces of their covenant. In each case, the unfaithful spouse came to a place of brokenness and repentance. Let us be clear: there cannot be reconciliation without repentance. Even God, in His infinite kindness and mercy, requires us to repent—to have a change of mind and heart—before we are reconciled to Him.

We have also known couples who couldn't reconcile. They need not feel a weight of condemnation. Jesus understood the gravity of the betrayal and made a necessary concession. We've watched God bless these friends as they recovered from divorce's wake.

If you have suffered a divorce, we encourage you not to allow it to define you. It is a part of your past, but it does not have to determine the landscape of your future.

The past is not yours. It belongs to God. The enemy of your soul will try to use your past to thwart God's plans for your future. Remember that God has given you today and that the choices you make today will shape your tomorrow—not your yesterday. If you've made poor choices, embrace the wisdom and power of God. Humble yourself through repentance and experience the wonders of His grace, which has the power to transform the bleakest of circumstances.

Am I Stuck?

Jesus' description of God's design for marriage must have been a radical departure from the norm. Rather than inspire His disciples, His words stressed them out. Look at their complaint:

Jesus' disciples objected, *"If those are the terms of marriage, we're stuck.* Why get married?" (Matthew 19:10 The Message, emphasis added)

Stuck? What a terrible perspective of married life! Yet, like the disciples, many of us view marriage as constricting and confining. How many single men and women are plagued by the fear of marrying the wrong person and getting stuck?

What we have learned is that marriage is not as much about finding the right person as it is about *being* the right person. Don't get us wrong, when searching for a spouse, it is important to seek godly counsel and the peace of the Spirit. But too often we believe Mr. or Ms. Right will miraculously fill all the gaping holes in our lives. No human being is up for that task. It's a role only God can fill. And you can't manage the condition of anyone else, reforming them into exactly what you think you need. What you can do is embrace God's process of refinement and become a man or woman who selflessly lays down your life for your current or future spouse. In the process of laying down your life, you will discover more fulfillment than if you'd sought your own interests.

Matthew 6:22 says that the light of the body is the eye. This means that your perceptions will be your reality. An "I'm stuck" outlook will limit what God can do in and through your marriage. If you perceive your marriage as a trap of hopelessness, that's what it will become. Your natural circumstances will ultimately be determined by your spiritual vision, and marriage is no exception.

You might be thinking, *John and Lisa, you're asking too much. You want me to lay down my life for my spouse? That's ridiculous. What about my needs, hopes, and dreams? Jesus wants me to be happy. What you've shared is just a nice thought, something to aspire to.* We can assure you, God does want you to be happy—but true happiness is the byproduct of a greater pursuit. Happiness comes from fulfilling a higher purpose, and any worthy purpose will require you to lay down your life. In the eradication of selfishness, we find true happiness. Marriage provides the perfect environment for this faceoff with self-centeredness.

"If two spouses," write Timothy and Kathy Keller, "*each* say, 'I'm going to treat my self-centeredness as the main problem in the marriage,' you have the prospect of a truly great marriage."[8] Self-centeredness keeps us from enjoying great marriages, which means the sacrifice of self is the key to enjoying marriage in its fullness. If you are struggling in your relationship with your spouse, self-centeredness is probably the source of the problem.

Day 5

The Largeness of Marriage

But Jesus said, "Not everyone is mature enough to live a married life. It requires a certain aptitude and grace. Marriage isn't for everyone. Some, from birth seemingly, never give marriage a thought. Others never get asked—or accepted. And some decide not to get married for kingdom reasons. But *if you're capable of growing into the largeness of marriage, do it.*" (Matthew 19:11-12 The Message, emphasis added)

While the disciples were focused on feeling stuck, Jesus was making a statement that had the potential to increase the limits of their existence. Jesus doesn't see marriage as a trap. He sees it as something that can *enlarge* your life.

It may seem that marriage diminishes the number and value of its participants; after all, isn't it two becoming one? Rather than diminishing or dividing, however, marriage causes increase. When two become one, there is multiplication in every area of life. Not until the creation of Eve could God give Adam the command to be fruitful and multiply— a decree that wasn't limited to making babies. The true potential of multiplication in marriage is impossible to quantify and too expansive to measure.

We can assure you that you wouldn't be reading this book (or any book by either of us) if it wasn't for our marriage. We would have lived small lives. I (John) am who I am today because of the grace of God and because of His gift of Lisa Bevere. Has our marriage always been easy? Absolutely not! But God has used our marriage to enlarge my life in every way.

I (Lisa) feel the exact same way and am so thankful for the way God has expanded my life through my husband. When we were first married, I was terrified of people, largely due to insecurity over having lost an eye to cancer when I was five. John knew my fear yet spoke to the gift of God on my life anyway. His encouragement helped release me into God's plan and a larger life, which to my surprise has involved a lot of ministry to people.

As we mentioned, when God charged us to multiply, He wasn't just talking about making babies. God realized that the joining of the man and woman (what appears to be the simple addition of *one plus one*) would create the opportunity for great multiplication. This principle holds true in every area of life: your career, your family life, your spiritual life, and more. In marriage, God has given us something that can push back our boundaries. If your life lacks blessing and multiplication, it's time to stop striving and start honoring and adoring your spouse.

It's Not Easy

A good military strategist will tell you that a significant element of every great battle plan is an intimate knowledge of the enemy and his schemes. (Why do you think football teams spend so much time watching video of their opponents' games?) When the enemy attacks marriages, especially Christian marriages, his intention is to divide and conquer. This knowledge should give us the motivation to withstand his schemes.

When we fight for our marriages, we are fighting for a God idea. Remember: God, not you, made marriage. Satan hates marriage because it's much more than a sexual connection—it's a spiritual union. Because your marriage possesses such significance, it will encounter opposition. But you must press on to reach the prize (see Philippians 3:14). Jesus never said it would be easy. In fact, He challenged us with these words:

> …"Not everyone is mature enough to live a married life. It requires
> a certain aptitude and grace." (Matthew 19:11 The Message)

A big part of maturation is the willingness to grow and learn. In his book *Sacred Marriage*, author Gary Thomas writes, "If you want to become more like Jesus, I can't imagine any better thing to do than to get married. Being married forces you to face some character issues you'd never have to face otherwise."[9] Jesus made it clear that married life is going to expose our immaturities, but if we're willing to grow in His grace (which requires humility, selflessness, and patience), we will eventually enjoy the largeness of marriage.

Contract or Covenant

People often view a marriage covenant as a contract. This is a problem. A contract is simply an agreement that is created to restrict movement. It implicitly says, "These are the boundaries. You will not break this agreement. If you violate our terms, then I have the right to get out of this." In other words, *I'm not stuck.*

Contract is also a verb, one the Merriam-Webster dictionary defines as "to reduce by squeezing or forcing together." That doesn't sound anything like what Jesus called the *largeness* of marriage. Marriage is supposed to enlarge our lives, not make them smaller.

God doesn't view marriage as a mere contract; He sees it as a spiritual covenant. It's an agreement that exclaims, "I am giving all of me to all of you. Everything I am and everything I have is yours, and everything you have is now mine. Everything we do will be multiplied, enlarged, and increased because of this beautiful exchange." Covenant gladly proclaims, "I'm stuck! And I'm happy about it!" That's enlargement.

Paul told the Ephesians:

Husbands...love your wives, *just as Christ loved the church...* (Ephesians 5:25, emphasis added)

Paul encouraged husbands to love their wives just as Christ loves the Church. This love is a covenant love that's much more than a contract. Husbands, aren't you glad that Jesus loves you even when you aren't very loveable? Aren't you glad that Jesus never views His relationship with you as just a contract, something He's "stuck" in? Our goal must be to imitate Jesus' love in our responses and attitudes toward our brides. (Paul doesn't stop there, by the way. He goes on to tell us to forfeit our lives for our wives. What a command!)

Keep in mind that in Ephesians 3, shortly before he wrote these words, Paul described the depth of God's love for His people. Only two chapters later, he commanded that the same kind of love be found within our marriages—that we love "just as Christ loved the church."

Our marriages are meant to model Christ's love for His Bride. Why would those who don't know Jesus want to be in relationship with Him if the relationships between His people are void of love, power, harmony, and commitment? Are you seeing why your marriage is so important? It's not just about you. It's about God's longing to reach the world with His love.

As we previously shared, true love for your spouse must be an overflow of receiving God's love for you. A love this profound cannot be fabricated. It must be received from the One whose love defies human understanding.

We will be the first to tell you that God's approach to marriage is not easy. There have been times in our marriage when we would have preferred to cut ties. It seemed like all hope was gone. But after being married for over thirty years, we are happier today than we've ever been, and we look forward to the next thirty years with hope and expectation.

A Tree of Life or a Tree of Death?

I (Lisa) love to garden, but John doesn't share my interest. He enjoys what the garden produces but not the toil it requires. Gardens are a lot of work, and they demand a lot of time. Fortunately for John, we live a few minutes from Whole Foods, so he doesn't need to get his hands dirty.

Much like gardening, cultivating a marriage requires a lot of time and energy. If we want our marriages to be healthy, there is no fast food option that will allow us to circumvent the necessary work, which is a good thing. Why? Because we value what we work for, and we need to value our marriages.

The good (and sometimes bad) news is that everything you plant in your marriage, you will harvest in different areas of your life. Earlier in this chapter, we explored the concept of our marriages as trees of life. The converse is also true. Your marriage can also be a tree of death.

Let's revisit our description of the two Eden trees:

Both of these trees enjoyed the same immaculate and uncontaminated conditions. Yet one tree spawned life, the other death.

God's institution of marriage is like soil, and your current or future marriage is like a tree. The original plan for marriage is good ground in which your union can grow, but the choice is yours: Will your marriage be a tree that produces life? Will your spouse, family, friends, and coworkers experience love, joy, and peace through its nourishment? Or will it offer discouragement, selfishness, and bitterness to those who eat its fruit?

Many of us have viewed the institution of marriage itself as the source of our problems. Others have sought to blame their spouses. Both perspectives expose a refusal to acknowledge and address the depravity of our own hearts. We hope this is no longer the case for you.

Before you continue this journey, a decision must be made. You must choose to believe that your marriage can and will become everything God has destined it to be.

Maybe you're inclined to think, *I'll believe it when I see it.* But belief in change always precedes the evidence of change, for all of God's promises are received by faith. The good news is that your marriage is not about you—it's all about Him. All you have to do is get over yourself and let God be God. After all, your marriage is His work of art. If you let Him, He will transform it into a beautiful masterpiece.

SEASONS OF MARRIAGE

For everything there is a season, a time for every activity under heaven.

—Ecclesiastes 3:1

Spring, summer, fall, and winter—four distinct seasons, each with its own joys and challenges. Your marriage is much the same. You will experience many seasons in marriage, passing through some more than once. In each season there are things to learn and opportunities to grow. Author and pastor **Charles Swindoll** shares these insights on the subject of seasons:

"I am glad God changes the times and the seasons, aren't you? ...The Master is neither mute nor careless as He alters our times and changes our seasons. How wrong to trudge blindly and routinely through a lifetime of changing seasons without discovering answers to the new mysteries and learning to sing the new melodies! Seasons are designed to deepen us, to instruct us in the wisdom and ways of our God. To help us grow strong...like a tree planted by the rivers of water."[10]

What would you say is one of the most wonderful seasons you have shared with your spouse? Briefly describe it and share why it is so special to you.

What would you say is one of the most challenging storms you have faced as a couple? How did you make it through, and what did the Lord teach you?

For encouragement, check out Ecclesiastes 3:11; Romans 8:28; 2 Corinthians 2:14.

Look around. What season would you say your marriage is currently in? What can you do to enjoy this season more?

_____

_____

_____

Pause and pray, *"Lord, what can we do to better enjoy the season of life we are in? Give us eyes to see things as You do. Help us to appreciate the good that we will reap in the future because of this season. In Jesus' name, amen."*

As the years pass, the unique "fingerprint" of your marriage becomes clearer. Take time now to be still and appreciate it. What makes your marriage special? Consider the gifts, talents, personalities, desires, goals, experiences, etc., of you and your spouse.

_____

_____

_____

Pray and ask the Holy Spirit to reveal the uniqueness of your relationship and what He specifically desires to do through you and your mate. Write what He shows you, and then take time to share it with your spouse.

GOD MADE MARRIAGE

God, not you, made marriage. His Spirit inhabits
even the smallest details of marriage....

—Malachi 2:15 The Message

In the beginning, before any other institution was established, marriage was made. In the words of pastor and masterful storyteller **Max Lucado**:

"God created marriage. No government subcommittee envisioned it. No social organization developed it. Marriage was conceived and born in the mind of God."[11]

God made marriage, and it is very important to Him—so important He desires to be intimately involved in every aspect of your relationship. His Word says, "The Spirit Whom He has caused to dwell in us yearns over us *and* He yearns for the Spirit [to be welcome] with a jealous love" (James 4:5 AMP).

Stop and think. Have you invited God's Spirit into every area of your marriage? Is His counsel essential to your daily plans? If you have only invited Him in occasionally, how is life different when you forget to involve Him?

_____

_____

_____

_____

_____

You have the privilege of talking with God anytime, anywhere, about anything. Are you struggling with fears, financial challenges, or difficulty communicating? Why not take your concerns to God in prayer? Carefully read these passages and write what the Holy Spirit speaks to you.

Philippians 4:6-7 • Matthew 6:25-34 • 1 Peter 5:7 • James 5:13-16

_____

_____

_____

_____

Matthew 7:7-11 • John 14:13-14 • 1 John 5:14-15

_____

_____

_____

_____

> *And we are sure of this, that he will listen to us whenever we ask him for anything in line with his will. And if we really know he is listening when we talk to him and make our requests, then we can be sure that he will answer us.*
>
> —1 John 5:14-15 TLB

God doesn't want your marriage to be a war zone. He wants it to be your *Eden*, a word that means a place of "pleasure and delight." What would you most like God to change in your marriage? After you answer, ask Him, "What is my part in seeing this happen? What needs to change in me?"

_____

_____

_____

REPRESENTING CHRIST

We're Christ's representatives. God uses us to persuade men and women to drop their differences and enter into God's work of making things right between them. We're speaking for Christ himself now....

—2 Corinthians 5:20 The Message

God, the Almighty Creator of all, has given us the privilege of partnering with Him to reveal His character and bring His will and ways to the earth. This is true for us both as individuals and as married couples. Author and missionary pastor **Rick Renner** explains:

"According to Paul's words in Second Corinthians 5:20, we are heavenly delegates—'ambassadors' who have been sent forth as Heaven's *representatives* to planet earth! As ambassadors for Christ, we are *the voice of Heaven.* As His representatives, we are authorized *to speak and act* on behalf of the Lord. And as Heaven's ambassadors, we are fully backed, fully funded, *fully defended*, and *fully assisted* by the authority and resources of Heaven!"[12]

You and your spouse are God's representatives to the world. He is "making His appeal" through you, entreating unbelievers to return to Him. So, how appealing are you? If you didn't know God and you saw a couple modeling your marriage, what aspects would cause you to be drawn to Him? What would turn you away from Him?

_____

_____

_____

_____

When the Body of Christ does not live and love well, people blaspheme the name of God (see Romans 2:24). Is the Holy Spirit showing you anything that needs to change—maybe an attitude, action, or aspect of your marriage that doesn't represent Him well? If so, what is it?

_____

_____

_____

_____

There's no need to feel condemned or hopeless! Whatever the Spirit shows you, He intends to change. All you need to do is surrender to Him and ask for His help.

There are areas in all our lives where we can grow and learn to represent the Lord better. How do we do it? Through the empowerment of His Spirit! As you personally receive His love, you receive the ability to love your spouse and those around you. Read these passages carefully and write what the Holy Spirit reveals to you about receiving and growing in His love.

Romans 5:5 • Ephesians 3:16-19 • 1 John 4:7-17

_____

_____

_____

_____

> *...God is love, and anyone who lives in love is living with God and God is living in him. And as we live with Christ, our love grows more perfect and complete....*
>
> —1 John 4:16-17 TLB

A NEW HEART

I'll give you a new heart, put a new spirit in you. I'll remove the stone heart from your body and replace it with a heart that's God-willed, not self-willed. I'll put my Spirit in you and make it possible for you to do what I tell you and live by my commands.

—Ezekiel 36:26-27 The Message

You may approach marriage with some fears or concerns. Perhaps personal experiences or the norms of our culture have caused you to view the gift of marriage as a burden. Perhaps you've hardened your heart in fear of failure. Perhaps you too have asked, "Am I stuck?" God wants to break through every barricade and give you a new heart, one soft and sensitive to His loving touch, so that you can flourish and fulfill His original plan.

There is nothing more important to Jesus than your heart. Carefully read His words in Luke 8:5-15. What is the Holy Spirit showing you in this passage? What is He revealing to you about your heart?

_____

_____

_____

_____

The parable of the sower is also found in Matthew 13:3-23 and Mark 4:3-20.

On your own, you cannot know what is in your heart. But the Lord can both *reveal* it and *heal* it.

Take a moment to meditate on these truths.

> ...For the LORD searches every heart and understands every motive behind the thoughts. If you seek him, he will be found by you....
>
> —1 Chronicles 28:9 NIV

"The heart is...a puzzle that no one can figure out. But I, GOD, search the heart and examine the mind. I get to the heart of the human. I get to the root of things. I treat them as they really are, not as they pretend to be."
—Jeremiah 17:9-10 The Message

Search me, O God, and know my heart; test me and know my anxious thoughts. Point out anything in me that offends you, and lead me along the path of everlasting life.
—Psalm 139:23-24

Pause and pray: "Lord, show me what is in my heart toward my marriage. Reveal it so that You can heal it, in Jesus' name." Get quiet. Listen for what He reveals. Write it down and surrender it to Him.

_____

_____

_____

Do you need a new heart, one that is willing to receive God's love and grace? Your heavenly Father would not hold you to His plan for marriage without making provisions to help you fulfill it. Why not ask Him for His help now? You can pray...

*"Father, thank You for the gift of marriage. Free me from whatever would cause me to perceive my marriage incorrectly and therefore miss out on its blessings. Give me a **new heart** that is soft and sensitive to your touch. Give me **new eyes** to see my marriage the way You see it. Help me to believe for the best, not expect the worst. Help us put You first in all we do. Thank You, Father. In Jesus' name, amen."*

THE LARGENESS OF MARRIAGE

..."Not everyone is mature enough to live a married life.
It requires a certain aptitude and grace. ...But if you're capable
of growing into the largeness of marriage, do it."

—Matthew 19:11-12 The Message

Enlarge. It means to increase, expand, broaden, or amplify. God, the Creator of marriage, wants to use your union as an instrument of enlargement. If you will yield to His masterful plan, He will work through your mate to make you more like Jesus and enable you to abound in all you do.

As iron sharpens iron, so one person sharpens another.

—Proverbs 27:17 NIV

It's said that in marriage opposites attract. There's strength in this: our differences are what enable us to be one. But in time, things that once attracted us can become the very things that repel us.

What are the top three qualities that first attracted you to your mate? What three things now frustrate you most? Is there any connection?

The Top 3 Things That Attracted Me   The Top 3 Things That Frustrate Me

_____   _____

_____   _____

_____   _____

Remember, your differences are meant to unite, not divide.

God's Spirit speaks words of wisdom to you and your mate, and His counsel isn't always given when you are praying together. Often He will speak to one of you separately about something both of you need to know. In order to make God-directed, God-blessed decisions, you need the insights He has deposited in each of you. Answer these questions honestly:

Am I open or closed to my mate's input (wisdom, direction, constructive criticism) in my life?

_____

In what areas am I open to their input? In what areas am I closed to it? Why?

_____

_____

_____

The mate God has given you is a major contributor to forming you into the person you are today. Name at least one positive change to your character or quality of life that has resulted from being in relationship with your spouse. How is God presently using them to enlarge your life?

_____

_____

_____

Have you ever thanked your spouse for helping sharpen and enlarge your life? If not, take time now to sincerely express your appreciation.

DISCUSSION QUESTIONS

*If you are using this book as part of the Messenger Series on
The Story of Marriage, please refer to video session 1.*

1 | From the beginning, marriage was a God idea. He made it and He has a plan and purpose for it. Carefully read Genesis 1:27-28, 31 and Malachi 2:15. Identify five things God intended for marriage. Next to these, write five counterfeit perversions Satan seeks to produce in their place.

GOD'S PURPOSES   SATAN'S PERVERTED COUNTERFEITS

_____   _____

_____   _____

_____   _____

_____   _____

_____   _____

2 | Godly marriages impact the lives of those they touch. Can you name a couple that is doing marriage well? How are they giving love a good name? What can you learn from them to help you guard the spirit of your marriage?

3 | In Matthew 19:6, Jesus said, "Because God created this organic union of the two sexes, no one should desecrate his art by cutting them apart" (The Message). When you hear the word *organic*, what comes to mind? How do these ideas help you see marriage in a fresh, positive light?

4 | In Matthew 19:10-12, Jesus said, "Not everyone is mature enough to live a married life. It requires a certain aptitude and grace. Marriage isn't for everyone. ...But if you're capable of growing

into the largeness of marriage, do it" (The Message). What does the *largeness* of marriage look like? How can we experience it?

5 | Marriage is holy and is meant to be a covenant between one man and one woman for life. What have you heard in this session that motivates you to fight for your marriage? What insights have given you a positive new perspective?

6 | Jesus said the light of the body is the eye (see Matthew 6:22). That is, the way you see things is vital—it becomes your reality. This is especially true in marriage. What will happen if you have an "I'm stuck" point of view?

Scripture says that we are in a spiritual war (see Ephesians 6:12-13 and 2 Corinthians 10:3-4). How does this help you see disagreements and difficulties with your spouse in a different light?

7 | *The Story of Marriage* is meant to help those who are engaged or single as well as those who are already married. Whichever description fits you, what do you hope to receive from this study?

If you are (or have been) married, what do you wish you would have known before you said "I do"? What words of wisdom can you offer to the unmarried in your group?

CHAPTER SUMMARY:

- God created the covenant of marriage before He created any other institution. He defined it, and its definition has never changed.

- Godly marriages are meant to be like trees of life. We are to model God's love as ambassadors through whom He offers restoration of everything once lost in Eden.

- Guard the spirit of your marriage by inviting God into every part of it. He will give you a new heart to receive and give His love and new eyes to see your marriage from His point of view.

- Self-centeredness is the greatest obstacle to experiencing and enjoying the amazing marriage God wants you to have.

- An attack on marriage is an attack on how God relates to His people.

- God created marriage to enlarge every area of our lives.

TWO

Begin with the End in Mind

Day 1

Have you ever noticed that most romantic movies and books only focus on the beginning of a love story? Think of your favorite romantic classic. (We realize this may be easier for some of you than others.) What is the storyline? Is it marked by the emotional tension expressed in the dance of courtship? Are you glued to the edge of your seat as the movie teases you with twists that keep the lovebirds from enjoying their climactic first kiss? Sure, there are temporary setbacks—a competitor, intense argument, or unexpected trauma—but we all know how it will ultimately end. Despite the problems that threatened to keep them apart, the starry-eyed lovers find a way to prevail and the story closes with, "And they lived happily ever after."

We know they lived *happily ever after*, but how? A wonderful beginning is the easy part. The hard work comes in crafting the story's middle and end.

It's evident that our culture has a lopsided obsession with how love stories begin. A couple may spend countless hours planning their wedding but very little time mapping out the years that will follow the ceremony. A bride may spend many hours searching for the perfect dress, while allotting only a few for premarital counseling. Consequently, the couple is largely unprepared when the fairy tale fades and they find themselves navigating a real relationship with very real problems.

Wedding days are meant to be full of hope, beauty, and celebration. However, a relationship's long-term hope and beauty are best realized when couples invest the same fervor in planning their happy endings as they do in celebrating their starts. *Happily ever after* is not something we stumble upon; it's a destination we are determined to pursue and careful to construct.

Look around and locate an object of beauty, one skillfully crafted by human ingenuity. Maybe it's a home, a car, or even the chair you're sitting on. Whatever it is, it's a well-thought-out work of craftsmanship. What you may not realize is that this object was actually constructed twice, once when it was creatively designed in the mind and again when the design was built. Cognitive design always precedes material construction. The first assembly requires a clear vision of the intended outcome; the second employs materials and labor to achieve it. Everything we build, whether it is as simple as a sandwich or as complex as a skyscraper, is first imagined before it can materialize.

You wouldn't dream of building a home without any blueprints. It would be a mess! Every beautiful home begins with a well-thought-out design. Only after the plan is drafted can the house be built, through hard work and with the right materials.

Blueprints are also essential in determining the cost of construction. Would you be comfortable building a home without first knowing how much it will cost you? Jesus posed this question when teaching us how we should build our lives:

> "But don't begin until you count the cost. For who would begin construction of a building without first calculating the cost to see if there is enough money to finish it? Otherwise, you might complete only the foundation before running out of money, and then everyone would laugh at you. They would say, 'There's the person who started that building and couldn't afford to finish it!'" (Luke 14:28-30)

What is true of constructing a building is also true of crafting a marriage. So, what type of marriage are you building? Have you counted the cost and come to terms with what building that marriage will require of you?

God doesn't want our marriages to end in pain or shame. He doesn't want us to quit before they're complete. Whether your marriage is just getting started or has been struggling for years, it's never too late to embrace God's plan. In Him, we discover the vision, tools, and power needed to construct marriages that reflect His greatness. The amazing truth is that God desires your happy ending—the completed construction of His masterpiece—even more than you do.

This chapter contains truths that will position you to plan, and therefore live, your story well. We will share what we did early in our marriage that established a solid foundation on which to weather life's storms. And we will equip and commission you to scribe a plan that will lead you to *happily ever after*. We will begin with principles and end with the very practical. This chapter is not just for the newlyweds or the not-yet-wed. Marriage veterans, you too can benefit from taking a fresh look at your relationship. We did!

God Begins with the End in Mind

It's foolish to enter a covenant relationship without first asking, "Why are we doing this and where are we headed?" Every covenant should have a corresponding vision. Take God, for example. He had a specific purpose in mind when He chose to make a covenant with Abraham.

Why do you think God chose Abraham to be the father of His chosen people? Whenever we ask this question, the most common answer is, "Because he had great faith." While faith is essential to partnering with God's plan, it's not why God chose Abraham. God chose Abraham because He knew that he would teach his descendants to follow the Lord:

> "For I have chosen him, *that he may command his children and his household after him* to keep the way of the LORD by doing righteousness and justice, so that the LORD may bring to Abraham what he has promised him." (Genesis 18:19 ESV, emphasis added)

When God chose this childless nomad, He looked beyond Abraham and saw his lineage. It was crucial to God that Abraham "command his children to keep the ways of the Lord" because God wanted to weave His story of redemption through Abraham's family line. He knew Abraham and Sarah would make mistakes, but He also knew they had the right raw materials. Whenever God establishes covenant with us, He is always thinking generationally because He has already visited tomorrow and knows what needs to happen today to get us there.

The covenant God made with Abraham expanded until it reached into our lives as well. Through faith, Abraham was transformed from a man without children into one with descendants as numerous as the stars. The man who was once a wanderer without a nation became a father of faith to all nations.

"...Abraham shall surely become a great and mighty nation, and all the nations of the earth shall be blessed in him..." (Genesis 18:18 ESV)

Our lives will look different than Abraham's, but the principle is the same. God looks for people who intentionally allow His covenant to spread through them. Your story is about more than just you and your spouse.

Only heaven will reveal the full impact of God's covenant expressed through your relationship with Him. He desires to reach every life that passes through you (your legacy) and every life that falls within your realm of influence. This means you have to embrace a vision that doesn't end with you and isn't confined to your limited understanding. God's intention for your story will always include the generations to come.

Day 2

Children of God

GOD, not you, made marriage. His Spirit inhabits even the smallest details of marriage. *And what does he want from marriage? Children of God, that's what....* (Malachi 2:15 The Message, emphasis added)

Children of God. That's what God is looking for from marriage. Does this mean that He is looking for more babies to populate the earth? Yes and no.

Malachi 2:15 does not say that God wants marriage to produce *children*. It says He wants it to produce *children of God*. God desires children—of any age—who will glorify Him and walk in His ways. Remember, we are His ambassadors. His goal is to reveal Himself to and through us.

The *Westminster Shorter Catechism* says, "Man's chief end is to glorify God, and to enjoy Him forever." We love that! *Glorify* isn't a common word used in everyday speech; due to its frequent use in Scripture, it is seen as something spiritual and obscure. *Glorify* simply means that we make God known. God's desire is to be made known through our lives, marriages, and legacies. And there is no catalyst like marriage for growing us into children of God.

Even if you never raise a child, God wants to use your marriage to make you a child of God. He wants to refine you into an agent of His glory and shape you into the likeness of your Father. Sharing your life with another person creates many opportunities for you to become more like God. We've discovered that more often than not, godly character isn't captured in the oceans of bliss. It's forged in the furnace of marital fire.

I (John) liken marriage to a furnace and our lives to an alloy, or blend, of precious metal. What does a blazing furnace do to an alloy? It exposes its impurities. My wedding ring may look like pure gold, but roughly fifty percent of it is composed of other substances. If I placed my ring inside a furnace, these impurities would be exposed. Similarly, the challenges we encounter in marriage—from trivial disagreements to profoundly difficult times—will reveal impurities in our lives. (Some impurities require more heat than others do to be revealed.)

When marriage relentlessly reveals our imperfections, it's easy to blame our spouses. After all, none of this was happening before we got married. When we find ourselves getting frustrated with our spouses because they are aggravating our "weaknesses," we should thank God that marriage is making us more like Jesus. Isn't that the ultimate goal?

Finding Purpose in Hard Times

We know our furnace analogy isn't exciting, but the journey to a happy ending is far from a fairy tale. At times your story may feel less like riding off into the sunset and more like climbing Mount Everest.

Those who brave the snowy slopes of the Himalayas to make the rigorous and challenging journey up Everest must do so with two things in mind. First, they must know that the undertaking will test the limits of their emotional and physical capacities. These daring men and women don't know all the particulars of the upcoming perils, but they know challenges are coming. Second, they must remember their goal: to ascend the highest mountain in the world. For them, victory is clearly defined as reaching 29,029 feet above sea level. Without awareness of this objective, these sojourners would quickly turn back as soon as they encountered their first significant obstacle.

The same applies to marriage. If we recognize that challenges are an inherent part of establishing our stories, then we will not be crushed when our emotional, physical, and spiritual capacities are tested. If we begin—and build—with the end in mind, we will not quit when we encounter major problems.

When teaching on spiritual maturity, Jesus said that *tribulation* and *persecution* would come against those who believe God's Word (see Mark 4:17). In the original Greek, these words are *thlipsis* and *diogmos*. *Thlipsis* is "trouble that inflicts distress, oppression, affliction, tribulation". [1] *Diogmos* is "a program or process designed to harass and oppress someone". [2] Neither sounds fun, but these forces facilitate our growth in God. Paul echoed Jesus' words:

We can rejoice, too, when we run into problems and trials [*thlipsis*], for we know that they help us develop endurance.

And endurance develops strength of character, and character strengthens our confident hope of salvation. And this hope will not lead to disappointment. For we know how dearly God loves us, because he has given us the Holy Spirit to fill our hearts with his love. (Romans 5:3-5)

Paul wrote that we should *rejoice* in problems and trials. Why? Trials create an opportunity for us to develop strength of character. Problems position us to become more like God. And we can take hope in the knowledge that God loves us and is always looking out for our best interests—so much so that He has given us His Spirit to fill our hearts with love even in the midst of our greatest struggles.

Scripture also makes it clear that God is not the one who authors our troubles. Satan is the one behind tribulation and persecution (see Mark 4:15 and James 1:12-13), but God will use the enemy's schemes against him. In the hands of the great Redeemer, what is meant to tear us away from God becomes a tool to make us more like Him.

Remember, the enemy hates marriage and everything it represents. He will do whatever he can to divide our unions and load them with seemingly unbearable trials. Having vision for our unions—and faith that God will bring us through difficulties—empowers us with hope to counter his assaults. God doesn't want us merely to survive the attacks against our marriages. He wants us to grow stronger through them. The key is to remember what we're fighting for (God's purpose), whom we're fighting against (Satan), and who is on our side (God's Spirit). Our faith and hope are actually strengthened through challenges—as long as we don't quit before He can finish His work in us.

Jesus' Happily Ever After

Jesus suffered more deeply than any other human being. He, the perfect God, became like us to suffer the pain and humiliation of an unjust mortal death. He made a way for us to be reconciled to God, yet the majority of humanity still rejects Him.

How was Jesus able to endure such immense pain and rejection? The answer is simple, yet awesomely profound: He never lost sight of His happily ever after. In His example, we find an outline for writing our stories:

> Keep your eyes on *Jesus*, who both began and finished this race we're in. Study how he did it. Because he never lost sight of where he was headed—that exhilarating finish in and with God— he could put up with anything along the way: Cross, shame, whatever. (Hebrews 12:2 The Message)

Jesus endured because He knew where He was headed. He looked through the suffering and saw the promise.

The English Standard Version phrases Hebrews 12:1-2 this way:

> …Let us run with endurance the race that is set before us, looking to Jesus, the founder and perfecter of our faith, who *for the joy that was set before him* endured the cross…. (emphasis added)

Did you catch that? "The joy that was set before Him." Was Jesus excited about enduring the cross? Absolutely not. He was so distressed He spent the night before His execution pleading with the Father for an alternative path. But Jesus had something that is lacking in many marriages. He had extraordinary vision. He could see past His circumstances and into the power and promise that would come through His choices. And what was Jesus looking to? We find the answer in Ephesians 5:

> ...He gave up his life for her [His Church] to make her holy and clean, washed by the cleansing of God's word. *He did this to present her to himself as a glorious church* without a spot or wrinkle or any other blemish. Instead, she will be holy and without fault. (verses 25-27, emphasis added)

We are Jesus' happy ending. We were the joy set before Him. Jesus endured the cross so that He could be reconciled with us, His Bride. The Church can now embrace Him unashamed of her former wretchedness, for in Him we have a new identity. This is the kind of perseverance, mercy, and unconditional love that should be present in our marriages. But it takes a vision—a hope for what might be—to sustain us through the challenges.

The writer of Hebrews continues with this exhortation:

> When you find yourselves flagging in your faith, go over that story again, item by item, that long litany of hostility he plowed through. *That* will shoot adrenaline into your souls! (Hebrews 12:3 The Message)

We all feel faint in our faith at times. That's why the writer of Hebrews says *when*, not *if*, you find yourself flagging in your faith. A great marriage requires nothing less than great faith, for to be *faithful* is to be *full of faith*. When your marriage is struggling, remember what Christ endured. Go over His story again. Your momentary difficulties, as painful as they may be, are nothing compared to the cross. When your faithfulness to your spouse is fading, recount Jesus' faithfulness to you. Remember all He endured to be reconciled with you. His example will shoot adrenaline into your soul!

Day 3

Believing for the Best

…I am God, and…there is none like me, declaring the end from the beginning…. (Isaiah 46:9-10 KJV)

It seems trite to write that "there is no one like our God," but too often we forget the power and truth of this statement. As children of God, we are invited to become like Him and to take on His nature. By faith we can become future shapers, fashioning our lives, children, and marriages by declaring the end at the beginning.

We've made it clear by now that *happily ever after* isn't something we stumble upon; it's something we intentionally build. The obvious next question is, "How do I build my happy ending?" You may have read these verses countless times, but read them again:

Now faith is the substance of things hoped for…. By faith we understand that the worlds were framed by the word of God, so that the things which are seen were not made of things which are visible. (Hebrews 11:1, 3 NKJV)

Our goal is to build a *happily ever after* that doesn't yet exist, and faith is the building material of what is not yet a reality.

God believed in us before we did anything worth believing in. He has great faith in you because He has great faith in Himself. He knows that His power can accomplish anything in your life. The only thing that will keep us from enjoying God's expansive power is unbelief, which is ultimately rooted in pride.

Pride manifests as arrogance or extreme confidence in our own ability. There is also a subtler form of pride that masquerades as self-loathing. In either form, it is a refusal to embrace all that God's magnificent power purchased through Christ's finished work on the cross. Jesus died to make you extraordinary. "We may be content," wrote C.S. Lewis, "to remain what we call 'ordinary people': but He is determined to carry out a quite different plan. To shrink back from that plan is not humility; it is laziness and cowardice. To submit to it is not conceit or megalomania; it is obedience."[3] We embrace the amazing life God offers us as we lift our opinions to the level of His provision.

Do you believe that you're worthy of a great marriage? Maybe these thoughts plague your mind:

I have too much baggage.
I don't come from a good family.
My parents didn't make it.
I've already made too many mistakes.
I need to be content with simply making it through.

In case you haven't noticed, God loves a challenge. But lack of faith will limit the effect of His power in our lives. A revelation of His greatness inspires us to be confident in Him, while at the same time keeping us humble. Humility opens the door to God's best for our lives. Isaiah 55:8-9 declares:

"My thoughts are nothing like your thoughts," says the LORD. "And my ways are far beyond anything you could imagine. For just as the heavens are higher than the earth, so my ways are higher than your ways and my thoughts higher than your thoughts."

You might as well accept that God is smarter, more perceptive, and more capable than you. "In God," wrote Lewis, "you come up against something which is in every respect immeasurably superior to yourself."[4] You must believe this if you want to access the materials essential to a great marriage.

Whatever we may think the potential of our marriages is, God has a vastly larger dream. Not only has He given it a lot of thought, but He has also made some great plans.

"For I know the plans I have for you," says the LORD. "They are plans for good and not for disaster, to give you a future and a hope." (Jeremiah 29:11)

This promise presents us with two choices: believe this statement is true and embrace God's vision for our marriages or assume He is a liar. When God looks into the future of your union, He sees the expression of His Son. The only way this vision will be realized is by receiving His grace (empowerment) through humility and faith. While *happily ever after* is something we plan for, it is not limited by our own strength. It is an expression of God's love accomplished by His Spirit working through us.

You might be thinking, *I'm pretty sure God has given up on my marriage. There is no hope for us. We have no vision for the future. We've lost that loving feeling.*

Is it possible you feel like this because you have labored in your own strength? Exchange your efforts and dreams for your marriage for God's. As you entrust your marriage to Him, He will take your dreams, infuse them with life, and plant a heavenly version inside your heart.

This means, husbands, He will empower you to love your wife the way Christ loves the Church, forsaking all self-centeredness. Wives, He will likewise empower you to respect your husband. In this way, both of you will be positioned to grow into the largeness of marriage.

The Bible makes it clear that without faith it is impossible to please God (see Hebrews 11:6). Why does God love faith so much? Because through faith in Him, we receive the power to become like Him, and there is no better existence than a God-like life. He takes pleasure in your pleasure—and we're not speaking of transient happiness. What we're describing is lasting joy, satisfaction, and fulfillment. God wants His best for your marriage, and His best is only established in the union that finds its substance in Him.

The Blueprint

Faith and hope are often confused for the same thing, but they're different. If faith is the building material of a great marriage, hope is the blueprint. To put it another way, hope is like a mold, and faith is what fills it. Without hope, faith is substance without shape, about as useful as building materials without a blueprint.

You'll remember that God hand-selected Abraham as the recipient of a covenant with a specific goal: that Abraham would instruct his descendants in the way of the Lord. Abraham was childless when God called him into this promise, but the Lord assured him that he would father a great nation.

Abraham was a man of extraordinary faith, one who Scripture says "never wavered in believing God's promise" (Romans 4:20). And yet in Genesis 15, we find that he battled discouragement before he stepped into the realm of faith.

> ...The LORD spoke to Abram in a vision and said to him, "Do not be afraid, Abram, for I will protect you, and your reward will be great."
>
> But Abram replied, "O Sovereign LORD, what good are all your blessings when I don't even have a son? Since you've given me no children, Eliezer of Damascus, a servant in my household, will inherit all my wealth. You have given me no descendants of my own, so one of my servants will be my heir."
>
> Then the LORD said to him, "No, your servant will not be your heir, for you will have a son of your own who will be your heir."
>
> Then the LORD took Abram outside and said to him, "Look up into the sky and count the stars if you can. That's how many descendants you will have!"
>
> And Abram believed the LORD, and the LORD counted him as righteous because of his faith. (Genesis 15:1-6)

We might have expected God to give Abraham a new measure of faith. But instead he gave Abraham's faith a vision to cling to. This strengthened his faith by giving structure to his hope. God invited Abraham outside to count the stars. The night sky painted a stellar blueprint for his faith as the countless stars above him transformed into the faces of children on the screen of his mind. Rather than simply telling Abraham his descendants would be as innumerable as the stars, God gave his destiny a constant, vibrant, physical illustration. Through this celestial show-and-tell, God's vision was imprinted on Abraham's imagination.

In the same way, God wants to use your imagination to impart His vision for your marriage, for where there is vision there is hope. This is why Paul encouraged us to cast down any imagination that exalts itself above the knowledge of God (see 2 Corinthians 10:4-5). You must protect the canvas of your mind because it will determine the nature and value of your actions. Think of your imagination as the drawing board for hope.

God has promised to fill us with hope, but how do we access it? It is in prayer that His Spirit infuses our spirits with transcendent hope:

I pray that God, the source of hope, will fill you completely with joy and peace because you trust in him. Then you will overflow with confident hope through the power of the Holy Spirit. (Romans 15:13)

God is our source of hope. If we ask, He will fill us with joy and peace, which is what we all want in our marriages. As we come to Him in humility, we will overflow with confident hope through the power of His Spirit. What a promise!

Proverbs 29:18 tells us we will perish without vision. Indeed, marriages without godly vision are void of life. So we dare you to dream big! As you prepare to script your dreams and goals, pray that God will awaken your heart to His plan.

Day 4

The Chinese Restaurant

When we were first married, we had a special spot where we would go to talk about our future. It was a little Chinese restaurant not far from our apartment. We were fresh out of college, and our finances were so tight that we would split a single order of mu shu chicken with an extra pancake and extra plum sauce. It was a quiet and humble, yet foreign, setting that encouraged a young couple to dare to dream of lands and hopes far away as they sipped tea.

At the time we didn't know much, but we were sure of one thing: we wanted to serve God together with all our heart, mind, and strength. We passionately desired to do life and family well. It would be correct to say we didn't know where we would journey to or land in life, but we knew how we wanted to travel. We wanted to live in such a way that God could establish a new legacy through us.

I (John) come from a great family background. My parents have been married for over sixty-five years. My father has faithfully loved and provided for our family, and my mom is the image of a classic homemaker. My parents have modeled many wonderful things about marriage and life for me, and I will be eternally grateful for their example.

I (Lisa) come from a very different family dynamic. John's parents seem perfect when compared to my family, which was ravaged by alcoholism, adultery, abuse, betrayal, greed, loss, and divorce. As John and I started our life together, it was obvious that I didn't have any experiential understanding of what a healthy family looked like; but I did have a desperate longing to be part of one.

As we talked in that Chinese restaurant, we knew we wanted to do marriage differently. Even though we had the utmost respect for the way John's parents had done marriage, their model wasn't right for us. We both knew there was more to marriage than what we'd seen; there was a divine calling upon the institution itself. Marriage was not only about us being together the rest of our lives; it was also about building an eternal legacy through our union. Of course this would include our children and our children's children, but it would also include impacting numerous other lives.

We began to paint a vision for our marriage. We asked one another questions, set parameters, and dreamed as big we could. We agreed that our primary goal was to serve God together and honor Him with our choices. Everything else would have to be run through that filter.

Over the course of thirty-two years of marriage, we have experienced seasons when the only reason we chose to stay together was because of our commitment to honor God. There was a period of time when I (Lisa) *felt* no love for John, and John actually told me he did not feel love for me. He threw himself into an intense travel schedule while I stayed behind with our young children.

To be honest, I saw no hope for love in the future. My soul was scarred by a season of wounding. I felt utterly abandoned both emotionally and physically. If I had ever considered divorce to be an option, I would have gladly taken that route. I had no vision for our marriage, just a faded shadow of what might have been. At one point I actually thought, *God, I will stay in this marriage as long as You promise me I won't have to live with John in heaven.* I felt so alone, and it is hard for minister's wives to share their pain with anyone.

I (John) too battled hopelessness in that time. I felt I could do nothing right in Lisa's eyes, and I believed my assessment was accurate due to the lack of respect and strong words with which she spoke to me. We were spiraling downward fast, and neither of us saw any potential for love, respect, and nurture to be restored.

The emotional and spiritual pain of that season seemed unbearable. It was awful, but it was only a season, and seasons change. A time of weeping may endure for a very long night, but we have God's promise that joy comes in the morning (see Psalm 30:5). Looking back, that time period seems surreal, like it happened to another couple. By God's grace, we remained faithful to our goal of honoring God. Through genuine repentance of our selfishness, coupled with obedience to godly wisdom, we have watched our marriage and love grow to a place of great strength.

One of the driving forces that kept us going through that difficult season was our view of life. We didn't see it as a seventy- or eighty-year time span; rather we saw it through an eternal perspective. Seventy or eighty years is but a vapor compared to eternity. Scripture teaches that what we do with the cross determines *where* we will spend eternity; however, the way we live as believers determines *how* we will spend eternity. Paul writes:

...We would rather be away from these earthly bodies, for then we will be at home with the Lord. ...For we must all stand before Christ to be judged. We will each receive whatever we deserve for the good or evil we have done in this earthly body. (2 Corinthians 5:8, 10)

It's clear Paul is not writing about unbelievers, for when unbelievers are absent from the body, they are not in the presence of the Lord. He is addressing those who have come into the family of God through the saving grace of Jesus Christ. We will stand before Him and give an account of the decisions we made and the manner in which we lived as believers. The judgments Christ renders will result in eternal rewards or eternal losses, ranging anywhere from having our life's labor burned up all the way to seeing it eternally rewarded and even reigning beside

Him throughout eternity. Knowledge of this fundamental doctrine kept us on course. Neither of us wanted to give an account before the throne of Jesus as to why we desecrated His art of the union of marriage. (For more on the Judgment Seat, see John's book *Driven by Eternity*.)

After our goal of honoring God, our second aim was to be more in love with each other at the end of our journey than we were at the beginning. This goal has compelled us to move through difficult times and love one another even when we haven't felt like it. C.S. Lewis wrote:

> Love...is a deep unity, maintained by the will and deliberately strengthened by habit; reinforced by (in Christian marriages) the grace which both partners ask, and receive, from God. They can have this love for each other even at those moments when they do not like each other.[5]

There have definitely been times when we have not liked each other. But God graced us to navigate those rough moments, and He will do the same for you. We like and love each other more today than we did on our wedding day—that's the truth! And we look forward to growing more in love with each passing decade.

God Is Taking Note

As we scribbled our dreams down on restaurant napkins, we talked about how we would raise the children we didn't even have. We discussed how we would handle discipline, allowances, chores, and sharing rooms. We talked about our legacy and the impact our decisions would have on our children and grandchildren. It was important to us that we impart spiritual and financial heritage to them (see Proverbs 13:22).

We imagined our future home. It wasn't important to us to have a large or elegant house; we wanted our home to be welcoming and warm, a place where people felt safe as soon as they stepped inside. We wanted it to be a fun place where our children would want to bring their friends.

We talked further about what we believed God had called us to do and how our callings would affect the dynamics of our marriage. We discussed the roles of women and the roles of men. We determined how we would manage our money and stay out of debt. On and on we talked until we looked down at what was in our hands and discovered that the scribble on napkins had turned into makeshift blueprints for the life we wanted to build.

We like to think that as we made our plans on scraps of paper, God was writing as well.

> Then those who feared the LORD spoke to one another, and the LORD listened and heard them; so a book of remembrance was written before Him for those who fear the LORD and who meditate on His name. (Malachi 3:16 NKJV)

There were many things we talked about in those early days that God remembered even when we had forgotten them, and He brought them to fulfillment. God records the conversations that occur between those who fear Him. As you map out a marriage that honors the Author of life, heaven takes note.

Day 5

Writing Your Vision

…"Write the vision; make it plain on tablets, so he may run who reads it." (Habakkuk 2:2 ESV)

Again, it's never too late to write your vision for your marriage. Feel free to write and rewrite it until you have crafted something that is distinct and easy to understand. A clear vision will give you the energy you need to run all the way to the finish line.

Please take some time to talk with your spouse (or future spouse) about your shared vision for your marriage. If you're single, start documenting your side of the vision now. Find a place where you can dream. Be specific with your desires and expectations. Determine your absolutes, and don't be afraid to dream big! This vision will be your north star in the days ahead.

Marriage is like a long-distance race with decades between the start and finish lines. Too many couples dream short-term. They dream of buying a house and raising a family, which are great goals, but neither will take you far enough. There's so much more. Keep dreaming!

Keep in mind that you and your spouse are running together, not competing against each other. You can't complete your course alone, so you need to work as a team. If you've had a rough start, take comfort in knowing that how you finish matters much more than how you began. Writing your plan is a way to define your finish line. You need to get the vision in front of you so you have something to run toward.

For still the vision awaits its appointed time; it hastens to the end—it will not lie. If it seems slow, wait for it; it will surely come; it will not delay. ...The righteous shall live by his faith. (Habakkuk 2:3-4 ESV)

Your God-breathed vision will go before you to forge a path to its fulfillment. If you keep the vision in sight, it will not fail you. There may be times when it seems that what God has spoken cannot be true. Your path may lead you to places you did not want or expect to go. Trust the process. God knows what needs to be stripped off you in order for you to complete the journey. The power of the One who inspired your vision will strengthen you in moments of need. But you must keep the vision before you.

Your plan should be a living, breathing, organic document. This means it should include two things:

Clearly defined absolutes

Certain beliefs and commitments will provide a necessary framework for your vision, things like "our marriage will honor God" or "we'll put each other's needs before our own." These are the things you consider to be non-negotiable. They will never change and should not be compromised.

Room to grow

A good plan doesn't provide answers to every question. It provides clarity. Only God knows all that lies before you, but you can gradually uncover aspects of His plan by the guidance of His Spirit. Over time your vision should grow in scope and definition, adapting to accommodate the advantages and challenges of each season. These areas of change might include the amount of time you invest in parenting as your children age or the ways you support each other's careers and callings.

Here are five practical steps we suggest you undertake to write your marriage plan:

1. Pray
Ask God to infuse your conversation, thoughts, and aspirations with His Spirit. Ask Him to provide the structure of hope that He wants your faith to fill.

2. Collect inspiration
Gather scriptures, articles, stories, photos, song lyrics, magazine clippings, and anything else that speaks to you.

3. Go somewhere you can dream
This place doesn't have to be elaborate or expensive. It can be as simple as the restaurant down the street or the park bench in your neighborhood.

4. Identify your goals
Dream big! Don't let yourself be limited by your current circumstances or what you've seen modeled in the past.

Topics to consider include: finances, parenting, family dynamics, personal development, spiritual growth, communication, rest and recreation, careers, household responsibilities, church involvement, community, and more.

5. Determine how to reach them
Once you've established your vision, take inventory: where are

you right now in relation to where you want to be? Assess your current status and strategize the standards, steps, or changes that will put—or keep—you on course.

Your plan will cover many seasons of life. With your goals in mind, answer these questions:

What will our marriage look like when we are...

> *Married without children?*
> *Raising young children?*
> *Parenting teenagers?*
> *Empty nesters?*
> *Enjoying our grandchildren?*
> *In our final season together?*

If you're single, dating, or engaged, how can you intentionally position yourself for the marriage you want in the future?

You've set goals for finances, parenting, and more. These are big-picture objectives, but they'll be supported by your standards, choices, and habits in the day-to-day. Think about these questions:

> *How and when will you handle your monthly budget?*
> *What kinds of vacations will you take, and how will you plan for them?*
> *What kinds of activities and entertainment will you enjoy together?*
> *How will you continue to date your spouse?*

How will you resolve differences with your spouse?

How will you spend time with your children?

How will you discipline your children?

Do you both want to pursue careers outside the home? If so, will this look differently in different seasons of your marriage?

How will you support each other's career or other major goals?

What kinds of educational opportunities will you pursue for yourself? For your children?

What kinds of recreational opportunities will be available to your children? How will you facilitate their interests and talents?

How will you invest in your physical well-being? (Exercise, rest, nutrition, etc.)

How will you invest in your spiritual well-being?

How will you raise your children in the knowledge of God?

How will your marriage and family benefit the world around you? (Your church, community, neighborhood, workplaces, etc.)

As we mentioned before, the specifics of your plan will likely change and evolve as you mature in wisdom and gather experience. That's okay. But it's essential that you establish a framework for your plan and commit yourself to standards that will be foundational for what's to come.

Climbing Everest

Imagine a couple getting on a plane. They are excited about their trip, but they have no idea where they're going. All they know is that this plane will take them to a great adventure. They assume that they are headed somewhere warm, so they have packed only beachwear and a few light sweaters in case it gets chilly in the evenings. After many hours of flying, they arrive at their destination—only to discover they have landed in Nepal. What they thought was a tropical excursion has turned out to be a frigid hike up Mount Everest. They clearly are not prepared to undertake such a treacherous and hazardous journey, so they immediately head home.

Many have viewed marriage as a trip to the beach, but it's more like a climb to a mountaintop: it's rewarding and exhilarating, but it's hard work. And while the illustration may seem a little ridiculous, the mortality rate of marriages is actually around twenty-five times higher than that of climbers of Everest.[6]

Why are Everest climbers so much more successful than married couples? Because they have vision for their journeys and they know what to expect. They're not shocked when they encounter thinner air, freezing temperatures, and relentless winds. Sadly, too many marriages fail because of unrealistic expectations and lack of vision. It's worth it to take the time now to establish your plan.

Doing It Well

As your story unfolds, God will expand the framework of your vision and add beautiful adornments to it, but He will never desecrate the life you are building with your spouse. Trials may feel like God's attempts to destroy your story, and you may be tempted to lash out at Him in anger or frustration. But know that God is not the author of your trials, and He works all things together for your good (see Romans 8:28). His grace and Spirit will never leave you, and He has promised that He will never allow you to go through a trial that you cannot overcome.

...God is faithful. He will not allow the temptation to be more than you can stand. When you are tempted, he will show you a way out so that you can endure. (1 Corinthians 10:13)

At times you may feel like everything is falling apart, but if you hold onto hope, you can and will weather the storms. When all is said and done, you will hear the words of the Master saying:

"Well done, good and faithful servant!..." (Matthew 25:23 NIV)

Isn't it interesting that the Master says "well done," not "perfectly done"? None of us navigate anything in this life perfectly. But we can do life, and marriage, *well*. This means that we navigate our marriages healthily and with humility, learning from our mistakes and pressing on in God's grace to receive His best. If you choose to walk this path, your marriage will do more than just survive. It will thrive. God will see you through.

...We desire each one of you...to have the full assurance of hope until the end, so that you may not be sluggish, but imitators of those who through faith and patience inherit the promises. (Hebrews 6:11-12 ESV)

God wants you to inherit His promises for your marriage. Lay claim to the hope His Spirit gives. Be patient with your spouse and have faith in what your marriage can become. You will be amazed by what God can do in and through two imperfect people. God is passionate about constructing marriages whose greatest stories are in how they end, not how they began.

A MASTERPIECE IN THE MAKING

*For we are God's masterpiece. He has created us anew in Christ Jesus,
so we can do the good things he planned for us long ago.*

—Ephesians 2:10

Everything God creates has purpose—including your marriage. Through His Spirit's personal involvement in your life, He desires to make your marriage a masterpiece of His grace.

Think back to when you were single or engaged. How did you envision marriage? What picture-perfect images and ideas did you have in your heart and mind?

_____

_____

_____

How is your marriage different than you envisioned?

_____

_____

_____

God's design is for marriage to be a covenant. This is a lifelong, "till death do us part" agreement. In covenant, each party surrenders and offers all its resources to the other. One person's difficulties become the other's, and each vows to protect and provide whatever their partner needs.

Authors and speakers **Bob and Audrey Meisner** have shared these insights concerning covenant:

"Covenant is a God thing. The Bible clearly speaks of the blessings of walking in covenant, which include favor with God, blessed finances, security and trust, long life and health and godly character! ...In a true covenant environment we feel free to admit our failures and recurring challenges in life because we know we won't be rejected for our honesty. Then our spouse feels free to speak the truth in love to help us overcome our failures, while walking with us through the difficulties. This is covenant living in Christ at its best."[7]

What is God speaking to you about covenant? Ask yourself, *Am I enjoying a covenant marriage? What am I willing to do to experience it?* Pray and ask the Spirit for His input and strength.

_____

_____

_____

God has a powerful purpose for your covenant marriage, reaching far beyond just you and your spouse. He wants your union, like Abraham and Sarah's, to send His love and truth far into the future. Ask yourself, and the Lord, *Who is my marriage impacting, and what effects is it leaving?*

_____

_____

_____

Pause and pray, "Holy Spirit, how can I intentionally extend Your covenant to my children, grandchildren, and those You have placed in my sphere of influence?"

_____

_____

_____

Get quiet before God. Listen for what He speaks now and in the days ahead. Write His instruction and ask for His grace to obey.

FORGED IN THE FURNACE

Friends, when life gets really difficult, don't jump to the conclusion that God isn't on the job. Instead, be glad that you are in the very thick of what Christ experienced. This is a spiritual refining process, with glory just around the corner.

—1 Peter 4:12-13 The Message

Marriage is a spiritual refining process, and God is the Refiner. While He is not the source of your problems, He will use them to make you and your spouse more like Jesus.

Let's face it. No one likes trials. If we could bypass them, we would. But there is value in the difficult path.

Take a moment and meditate on these truths about the benefits of trials. We've tailored them to directly address your marriage.

"But [God] knows every detail of what is happening to me [and my spouse]; and when he has examined me, he will pronounce me completely innocent—as pure as solid gold!"

—Job 23:10 TLB

You have purified [my spouse and me] with fire, O Lord, like silver in a crucible. ...We went through fire and flood. But in the end, you brought us into wealth and great abundance.

—Psalm 66:10, 12 TLB

Consider it a sheer gift, [husbands and wives], when tests and challenges come at you from all sides. You know that under pressure, your faith-life is forced into the open and shows its true colors. So don't try to get out of anything prematurely. Let it do its work so you become mature and well-developed, not deficient in any way.

—James 1:2-4 The Message

...Trials will show that your faith is genuine. It is being tested as fire tests and purifies gold—though your faith is far more precious than mere gold. So when your faith remains strong through many trials, it will bring you [and your spouse] much praise and glory and honor....

—1 Peter 1:7

Briefly describe a furnace of affliction (a conflict) you and your spouse are currently facing.

_____

_____

_____

What is the Holy Spirit showing you about you, your spouse, and your situation through the above scriptures?

_____

_____

_____

Knowing what is wrong with your mate will not help you change. Change begins by knowing what needs to be addressed in you. Pause and pray, "Holy Spirit, what's going on in my heart and mind? What do You seek to change? What do I believe about myself that is not true? Help me hear Your voice and obey Your commands. In Jesus' name."

The truth the Holy Spirit is revealing about me is...

_____

_____

_____

The actions the Holy Spirit is prompting me to take are...

_____

_____

_____

FAITH, HOPE, AND HUMILITY

May God, the source of hope, fill you with joy and peace through your faith in him. Then you will overflow with hope by the power of the Holy Spirit.

—Romans 15:13 GW

Faith provides the building blocks for a fantastic marriage, and hope is the blueprint to bring it about. God, the source of hope, has faith in you and your spouse. As you trust in Him, He will give you His blueprint for your marriage and empower you to experience the marriage of your dreams.

In his book *Abraham, Or The Obedience of Faith*, pastor and author **F. B. Meyer** explains:

"Faith is the tiny seed which contains all the rare perfumes and gorgeous hues of the Christian life, awaiting only the nurture and benediction of God. When a man *believes*, it is only a matter of education and time to develop that which is already in embryo within him... Faith unites us so absolutely to the Son of God that we are One with Him forevermore; and all the glory of His character...is reckoned unto us."[8]

So what is faith? Where does it come from? And how can you see it grow stronger in your life? Carefully meditate on these passages and write what the Holy Spirit reveals to you.

Romans 1:11-12; 10:17; 12:3 • Hebrews 11:1, 6 • Ephesians 2:8 • Colossians 2:6-8

_____

_____

_____

Along with faith, you need hope, a God-given blueprint for your union. Pause and pray, "Lord, deposit in me and my spouse Your divine diagram for our marriage. As You gave Abraham an illustration in the stars of the sky, inscribe on our hearts an image we can understand and remember forever. In Jesus' name." Look, listen, and write what the Lord reveals.

There is one key virtue you need in order to receive faith and hope. It's *humility*. Humility says, "I can do nothing without You, Lord, but I can do all things through You." When you possess a heart of humility, the door to God's best for your marriage is thrown wide open!

Nineteenth century author and pastor **Andrew Murray** said, "Jesus came to bring humility back to earth, to make us *partakers* of it, and by it to save us. ...His humility is our salvation. His salvation is our humility. ...*It is only by the indwelling of Christ in His divine humility that we become truly humble.*"[9]

Carefully meditate on these verses. What is God revealing to you?

Matthew 11:28-30 • **John 13:1-17** • **Philippians 2:1-11** • **James 4:6** • **1 Peter 5:5**

----

*...Accept life with **humility** and patience, making allowances for each other because you love each other. Make it your aim to be at one in the Spirit, and you will inevitably be at peace with one another.*

—Ephesians 4:2-3 Phillips

DREAM BIG TOGETHER

Two can accomplish more than twice as much as one,
for the results can be much better. ...Three is even better,
for a triple-braided cord is not easily broken.

—Ecclesiastes 4:9, 12 TLB

Living and experiencing the largeness of marriage—this is God's divine design for every husband and wife. With His Holy Spirit at the center of your union, you and your spouse will be positioned for greatness!

Do you want to live large? Take time to dream big. At the end of this chapter, you'll be equipped to script a vision for your marriage. Right now, you can prepare for this special vision-casting time.

Name a couple places where you and your spouse enjoy being together, relaxing places where you are free to dream.

_____

_____

_____

Discuss your responses, then pick one or more places where you can schedule a series of dreaming dates.

Dreaming together allows you and your mate to honestly share from your hearts and envision the amazing things you can do together by the strength, wisdom, favor, and provision of God. "What can you do as a couple to make your pursuits more effective?" ask authors **Bill and Pam Farrel**. "Be deliberate. ...To know whether you are making any headway on a dream, you need to write a set of goals that explain how to get to the dream. A goal must be *specific...realistic...*[and] *achievable with God's help.*"[10]

We'll discuss goal planning more during the next day's reading. For now, what dreams are in your hearts? Think about your desires regarding your relationships with each other, raising a family, financial security, education and careers, buying or building a home, retirement, etc.

My greatest dreams for our marriage are...

_____

_____

_____

Once you share and write your dreams, ask your spouse to share theirs and write them down.

My mate's greatest dreams for our marriage are...

_____

_____

_____

What aspects of these dreams overlap? Where is there common ground? Discuss these together.

The greatest dreams we share for our marriage are...

_____

_____

_____

Remember, "God can do anything, you know—far more than you could ever imagine or guess or request in your wildest dreams!"(Ephesians 3:20 The Message). Submit your dreams to the Lord in prayer and ask Him to begin showing you the specific steps you can begin to take toward them.

WRITE YOUR VISION

"...Write the vision, and make it plain upon tablets..."

—Habakkuk 2:2 KJV

Now that you and your spouse have begun to dream together, the next step is writing your vision. Having a vision means having a realistic dream for your marriage and for what you and your mate can become together by God's direction and grace.

Author, professor, and family counselor **H. Norman Wright** offered valuable insights on the topic of vision:

> "**Vision** could be described as *foresight*, with the significance of possessing a keen awareness of current circumstances and possibilities, and of the value of learning from the past. Vision can also be described as *seeing the invisible and making it visible*. It's having a picture held in your mind of the way things could or should be in the days ahead. Vision is also *a portrait of conditions that don't yet exist*. It's being able to focus more on the future than getting bogged down with the past or present. Vision is the process of creating a better future with God's empowerment and direction."[11]

A successful marriage vision has absolutes. Jot down some non-negotiable standards that you and your mate are willing to guard without compromise.

_____

_____

_____

_____

_____

These may include things like avoiding strife, staying out of debt, always being willing to forgive, never putting each other down, etc.

Reread Wright's description of vision. What does this speak to you? What are some **short-term goals** for your marriage, things you and your mate would like to attain in the next year?

_____

_____

_____

What's your **medium-range vision** for marriage? What goals would you like to achieve in the next five to ten years? Remember, be specific and realistic, and focus on what you want to see.

_____

_____

_____

What is your **long-range vision** for your marriage? What specific goals would you like to attain in the next twenty to thirty years? Consider retirement, grandkids, ministry or vocational opportunities, travel, etc.

_____

_____

_____

> _"But these things I plan won't happen right away. Slowly, steadily, surely, the time approaches when the vision will be fulfilled. If it seems slow, do not despair, for these things will surely come to pass. Just be patient! They will not be overdue a single day!"_
>
> —Habakkuk 2:3 TLB

DISCUSSION QUESTIONS

If you are using this book as part of the Messenger Series on
The Story of Marriage, *please refer to video session 2.*

1 | Many married couples live in survival mode. But God doesn't want marriages that barely survive. He wants marriages that thrive! Take a few moments to share why it is important to expand your vision for your marriage beyond just you and your spouse.

2 | Without question, you will face difficulties in marriage. You and your mate are two individuals in the process of becoming one. Hebrews 12:2-3 gives us a proven plan for dealing with difficulties. Carefully read this passage and identify God's strategy for bringing you forth from the furnace of refinement like pure gold.

> *Keep your eyes on* Jesus, *who both began and finished this race we're in. Study how he did it. Because he never lost sight of where he was headed—that exhilarating finish in and with God—he could put up with anything along the way: Cross, shame, whatever. And now he's there, in the place of honor, right alongside God. When you find yourselves flagging in your faith, go over that story again, item by item, that long litany of hostility he plowed through. That will shoot adrenaline into your souls!*
>
> —Hebrews 12:2-3 The Message

3 | Pride keeps us from enjoying God's best for our lives. How have you allowed pride to limit your vision for your marriage? What changes should you make to realize the marriage God has in store for you?

4 | Happy, healthy marriages that are growing into greatness have vision. A good vision is supported by a specific, realistic plan. Each couple customizes their own plan, and both husband and wife commit to seeing it fulfilled. Name some of the areas of marriage where having a detailed vision is necessary. Why is it so helpful and vital to record a specific plan? Why is it important for the vision to adapt and adjust with time?

Leaders: Have your group read Habakkuk 2:2-3; Proverbs 29:18.

5 | In Matthew 25:23, the servant who is "good and faithful" is commended for stewarding his masters entrustments "well." Doing marriage perfectly is different from doing it well. How can an expectation of perfection keep us from doing marriage well? What does doing it well mean for our standards? Our attitudes? Our responses to mistakes?

CHAPTER SUMMARY:

- Your story of marriage is about more than you. It is about every life that you and your spouse will touch during your lifetimes, and it reaches into your legacy for generations to come.

- Marriage creates an ideal environment for men and women to be shaped and refined into the image of Christ. This brings God great glory, making Him known.

- Faith is the building material of a wonderful marriage that is not yet a reality. Hope is the blueprint—or God-given vision—that faith builds.

- Humility opens the door to God's best for our lives. Through humility we receive God's grace (empowerment) to experience the largeness of marriage He designed.

- Regardless of the current condition of your marriage, it can grow into a happily ever after.

- Write a vision for your marriage: a living, breathing plan that grows with time and includes your hopes, dreams, and non-negotiable standards.

THREE

Clear the Decks

Clear the decks: (verb) Prepare for a particular event or goal by dealing with anything beforehand that might hinder progress[1]

Day 1

This nautical term was originally a command given aboard ships approaching battle. When thus instructed, sailors knew to remove any tools, ropes, or other gear that might hinder them from freely moving about the vessel.[2] Today the term applies to any preparation that positions us for unencumbered action.

In the last chapter, we talked about your marriage in terms of a working, living blueprint. The purpose of this chapter is to address any issues that might hinder you from moving forward and experiencing the largeness of marriage. The intentional act of clearing a ship's deck serves to keep the ropes from tangling with one another. If the deck is cluttered with debris or disorganized, it is easy, in hard times or rough seas, to trip over something that you could easily step around when sailing is smooth.

We love the idea of positioning you to sail into your future carrying all that will sustain you, while at the same time dumping overboard anything that would weigh you down or anchor you to the past. Far too many have not only "tripped on the decks" and been hurt, but they've also fallen overboard and been lost at sea.

God's design for marriage is flawless. Yet marriage seems to highlight each spouse's flaws like no other institution. Rather than wait until you are navigating a vessel that is desperately off track—with ripped sails, lost cargo, leaking holds, and frayed ropes—we want to soundly position you to *make way*.

Staying with our nautical imagery, a refusal to soundly address foundational relationship issues could be likened to putting out to sea with a cork plugging a leak in the bottom of your ship. It will work for a while, but when enough pressure is applied, it will not hold.

We don't want you tripping or sinking. We want your marriage to be an ark that can withstand any storm you encounter. As you worked on your marriage blueprint from the previous chapter, you may have already recognized some issues you need to address before you can move forward with what you envisioned. So let's go after every compromising flaw that is rooted in selfishness, pride, and offense. Let's cut ourselves free from every tethering curse and binding fear and let hope be our anchor.

Our Beginning

We know this clearing of the decks is important because this was not how we began our journey together. We didn't really listen during premarital counseling. When our counselor tried to give us advice about navigating conflicts and stormy waters, we thought, *Fight? We'll never fight! God put us together. This advice is for people who aren't in love like we are. We are not those people. God's hand is on our lives.*

After only a few weeks of marriage, the problems started. It didn't take long to realize how wrong we had been. We had entered marriage with visions of perfect spouses, but soon we became increasingly aware of each other's every flaw. We began to work hard at changing each other. As a result, our blissful marriage became a battleground between two very strong-willed people. Sparks flew as iron attempted to sharpen iron.[3]

We still didn't realize that our union was actually weak and fragile. Yes, we were deeply committed to each other, but we thought too highly of our own character, specifically in the areas of patience and selflessness. We had more issues than we would have cared to admit, and even what was good needed fortification to withstand the challenges to come.

Instead of allowing God to clear our decks, we just wanted to *deck* each other. The couple who believed they were a literal match made in heaven had fallen from bliss. We still put on a good face in church, but our home life started to look more like a scene from *WWF Monday Night Raw*.

During our first year of marriage, there was a time when we were engaged in what some would call "intense fellowship." John didn't want me (Lisa) to leave the room, so he told me to sit down on our bed. I wanted out of the room before I could say anything else I'd regret in the morning. John told me to sit down, but I was already in motion when he attempted to sit me back down on the bed to hash things out. The combination of my forward motion and John's shove landed me on the floor.

I jumped to my feet with a floor lamp in my hand. John stared at me in disbelief, a look of terror on his face. "What are you going to do with that?" he asked.

"I don't know," I muttered. The ridiculousness of the scene created an opportunity for both of us to calm down and talk through the issue, but the root of the problem went unresolved.

A few days after this episode, I was having lunch with one of my friends. She had been married longer than I had, so I felt somewhat comfortable opening up to her about my marital struggles. But rather than blurt out the details of the floor lamp incident, I decided upon a subtler approach. I casually asked, "Have you ever been in a disagreement with your husband and suddenly found yourself with a floor lamp in your hands?"

She looked at me like the question was absurd. "No!"

I quickly replied, "Me neither!"

I was obviously lying. My friend could probably infer that my supposedly random question was a cry for help. But marital pretenses kept us from taking the conversation any further.

John and I felt like we had nowhere to go. Major issues were developing in our marriage, but we didn't know who to turn to. At church we hid our struggle and masked our pain. We knew our relational friction was escalating, but we didn't know how to respond to it. The hopelessness and shame of our situation caused things to go from bad to worse. Consequently, the tension in our home became unbearable.

Then it happened. Our conflict reached an all-time high when I (John) struck Lisa. Before this incident, we had been physical—I had shoved and pushed her—but this was the first time I had struck her. Immediately, I realized what I had done and was completely horrified by my behavior and consumed with remorse. Lisa struck back and then locked herself in the bathroom. We both went to bed that night feeling something had been lost.

The next morning as we both got ready to leave for work, Lisa was silent and increasingly distant. It seemed our relationship was devoid of all sanctity and trust. Both of us were working full-time, and as the workweek passed, the distance between us widened. Lisa was working in sales at the time, and she began intentionally staying out late, checking on the stores in her region to avoid contact with me. When she finally came home, she refused to talk or eat dinner with me and headed straight to bed to read. I was looking forward to the weekend so that we could finally settle what had happened.

My Vow

As a young woman, I (Lisa) made a vow that if my future husband ever hit me, I would leave him. I was raised in a volatile home and was terrified of finding myself in another abusive situation. When John hit me, I was reminded of my vow and confronted with a potentially life-altering decision. Could I remain in my marriage? Could I love and commit myself to a man who had struck me?

The people I worked with knew something was deeply troubling me. One of my supervisors guessed what had happened. She encouraged me to leave John immediately, no questions asked. I was waiting for the weekend to come so I could lock John out of the house. In addition to talking to my co-workers, I was reading Dr. James Dobson's book *Love Must Be Tough*, which inspired me to elevate the situation to a crisis.

When John came home that evening, he could not get into the apartment. I had locked the deadbolt, which was only accessible from the inside. He did not have a way to get in. This was before cell phones, so he stood outside and called out, "Lisa, I'm home. Please let me in!" I eventually opened a window to inform him that I knew he was home, but that he would need to find another place to stay for the night. John was in complete disbelief. After a while, he realized that he was not getting in, so he decided to stay the night with a friend under the guise of prayer and fasting.

Now that I had the place to myself, I decided to have a serious conversation with God. I think my opening prayer went something like this: "All right, God, I've got some ideas for You. While John is away, he needs to have a revelation of how horrible he has been toward me. Maybe You could give him a bad dream or scare him with a lightning strike. Just please don't kill him because I don't have enough life insurance on him."

But no matter how much I prayed about John, the only person God would talk to me about was me. God wasn't interested in discussing John's issues with me. He wanted to address the condition of my heart. He told me, "Lisa, you need supernatural intervention in your marriage. And if you want supernatural intervention in your marriage, you're going to have to act supernaturally. That means you forgive when you don't think it's deserved."

"Lisa," God kept saying, "you hold an account against John."

Keeping an Account

When John and I fought, we didn't just fight about the issue at hand. We used ammunition from our months of marriage to belittle and discredit each other. An ever-growing record of offenses, condemnation, and bitterness was the foundation for every disagreement. Even small arguments evolved into battles of what felt like epic proportions.

I, the biggest culprit in these drawn-out conflicts, was unwilling to forgive John his past offenses. Because of the hurt I had carried into our relationship, I was scared that if I canceled his debts, I would jeopardize my emotional and physical safety. Yet God told me that while John was far from perfect, he deserved my forgiveness.

I kept trying to direct God's attention back to John, but He wasn't cooperating. I pleaded, "Why do I always have to change? I hope You're telling John to do the same thing because he's not going to change unless You tell him to."

But through all of this, God was revealing the depravity of my own heart. Pride and selfishness soon reared their ugly heads. I found myself thinking about how people would respond if John and I weren't sitting together or holding hands at church on Sunday. I decided I would allow him to come home just in time to get dressed and ride with me to church so we could keep up appearances. I wasn't concerned about John or our relationship. I was concerned about what other people thought of us. My pride was keeping me from experiencing the transforming effect of God's grace right where I needed it most.

Finally I broke and let God have His way in my heart. Even in the wake of John's heinous mistake, I chose to acknowledge my part in what had transpired. As soon as I humbled myself, God's grace entered in. Humility always opens the floodgates of grace:

…"God opposes the proud but gives grace to the humble."
(1 Peter 5:5 ESV)

It became evident to me that I could not change John. Only God could do that. But I could allow God to change me.

John came home from that weekend away a different man. After God dealt with him in the first years of our marriage, he never struck me again—and it's now been almost three decades. Our union was transformed as both of us responded in humility before God and each other with hope for complete restoration and reconciliation.

The Moral of the Story

We wish we could say the wounds from that season of our lives healed overnight, but they didn't. The next two years of our marriage continued to be marked by great emotional turmoil and struggle as we tried to learn how to live together in a way that honored God. We had heard advice ranging from both of us being the boss to Lisa utterly disappearing in voice and role.

In our immaturity, we frequently lashed out at each other when God was doing a work in our individual lives. We emerged from our first four years of marriage feeling very broken. In some ways, we lived in the aftermath of our mistakes. There was even physical evidence of our failures around us, including a damaged refrigerator and a replaced window. But God didn't lose hope in us. He was redeeming our mistakes by turning them into opportunities to clear the decks. What the enemy meant to destroy our marriage, God used as a foundation for what was to come.

Though we have always said we had struggles, we have never gone into this much detail in our teachings. We are sharing more information now not to excuse our behavior, but to encourage you that change can happen. At the same time, we know that not all abuse has a happy ending, and we are not encouraging any woman or man to stay in a situation in which they or their children are unsafe. If this is you, get to a place of safety. Don't be ashamed. Be safe and get the help you need. More on this in a moment.

During these challenging years, our marriage looked utterly hopeless; yet thirty years later, we are enjoying life together more than ever before. Our marriage is amazing, which is truly a testament to God's miracle-working power. This is not to say that we have not experienced additional valleys along the way. But this we know: as we have chosen to love, God has been faithful to bring us through each one.

We don't know what your relationship looks like now, but we can assure you there is hope! Turn your heart toward God and allow Him to deal with you. You cannot change your spouse, but He can. Turn the responsibility over to Him. He will begin a beautiful change if you'll allow Him to.

A Word about Abuse

We want to make this clear. Husband, it is never okay for you to get physical with your wife. The Bible says you are to honor her as the weaker vessel (see 1 Peter 3:7). Your wife's emotional or even physical attacks do not warrant similar response. Walk away if you must. Do not respond physically, even if it is only in retaliation to her attacks, or you will forfeit your wife's trust. She will no longer feel safe in your arms. If you have been abusive toward your wife, immediately repent before God and ask your spouse for forgiveness.

Wife, your husband's natural desire is to protect you. God gave many men superior strength for this very purpose. You may consider physical attacks on your husband to be trivial fits of anger, harmless as long as they don't inflict physical damage. But to him, your attacks are devastating. Right or wrong, men are wired to respond physically when they are attacked. We do not want to provoke or evoke the worst in one another; we want to bring out the best. If you have been abusive toward your husband, repent and immediately cease such behavior.

Maybe you grew up in a family culture of violence. Perhaps your family defaulted to verbal, emotional, or physical abuse. We want you to know this is never a healthy way to resolve conflict. Christian counseling can give you the tools you need to resolve the challenges of life and family in a healthy way. Many churches offer small group studies on these topics. Never be ashamed to seek professional and spiritual help.

This goes for both husbands and wives: if your spouse feels unsafe around you, remove yourself from their proximity and work to regain their trust. Do not try to force conversation in any setting where they feel at risk. If you do, things will only escalate, and you will most likely do something you will later regret.

Day 2

Offense

To forgive is to set a prisoner free and discover
that the prisoner was you.
—Lewis B. Smedes

The first thing that needs to be cleared from the decks in your marriage is offense. Because offense is so toxic, we will spend much of this chapter discussing this one issue.

A refusal to forgive robs freedom and hinders our passion. It takes perverted pleasure in the pursuit of revenge—an endless quest accompanied only by misery. The act of forgiveness is an act of liberation for both the offender and the offended.

Many believe forgiveness should be withheld until adequate recompense is received. How many of us have said, "I'll forgive them when they change"? But in God's kingdom, forgiveness is not optional. It's the only way of life. The more we forgive, the more we become like our Father in heaven. If we are going to be agents of His greatness, we must embrace the power of forgiveness.

Paul charged us:

Make allowance for each other's faults, and forgive anyone who offends you. Remember, the Lord forgave you, so you must forgive others. (Colossians 3:13)

This is often hard to swallow. It is a command, not a suggestion. And there are no conditions or exceptions given. God tells us to forgive anyone who offends us. End of story.

We often make liberal allowances and excuses for our own faults and expect others to do the same. Yet we find it much more difficult to forgive the faults of others, especially our spouses. But anyone who is unable to forgive has forgotten what they have been forgiven of. Many of us become self-righteous and forget that we all deserved to spend eternity in hell. Our offense toward God was so severe that He had to sacrifice His only Son to reverse its effects. Christ spoke His pardon from the cross, when bitterness would have been a far easier choice. He forgave us before our behavior was worthy of His forgiveness, and we are to do the same for others.

We probably don't have to convince you that your spouse isn't perfect. No one is! But mistakes create opportunities for us to extend God's grace. Our willingness to forgive is one of the greatest evidences of Christ within us.

Releasing the Hurts

When we were first married, I (Lisa) was among those guilty of saying, "I'll forgive you when you change." Until John altered his behavior, my running list of his offenses would continue to grow. I thought withholding forgiveness would motivate him into transformation, but it left him feeling condemned, hopeless, and disempowered.

Everything changed when God showed me how He forgives. His forgiveness is not a reward for modified behavior. It is a vote of confidence. As God renewed my understanding of forgiveness, He replaced the words in my mouth with ones that reflected His heart: "I believe you want to change, and I forgive you."

At the time, I didn't understand how important it was for me to forgive John. I later realized that my bitterness toward my husband was warring against his ability to change, for Jesus said:

"If you forgive anyone's sins, they are forgiven. If you do not forgive them, they are not forgiven." (John 20:23)

For centuries this verse has been misappropriated and twisted into a tool to propagate fear and oppression. This was not Jesus' intention. When we study the entire body of His ministry, we can understand the purpose and significance of these words. Jesus, more than anyone else, understands the power of forgiveness, for through it He reconciled the irreconcilable.

Remember, according to 2 Corinthians 5:17-20, we are the ministers of reconciliation through whom God makes His appeal to the world. We are meant to affirm and extend the forgiveness offered in Christ. When we instead choose to maintain an offense, we cease to declare God's hope and instead agree with the one who is called the accuser of the brethren. We articulate condemnation to those whom God wants to offer a new start. In his commentary on Jesus' words, G. L. Borchert put it this way: "There needs to be a recognition of the significant role that declarations of forgiveness can have in freeing people to set aside their past sins and feelings of guilt and turn their attention to the joy of living with the risen Christ under the direction of the Holy Spirit."[4]

Forgiveness is a divine act. No other virtue requires such a great sacrifice of self. It is a conscious choice of vulnerability instead of vindication. But in the sacrifice of self we find God's embrace. By choosing forgiveness, we refuse to worship our feelings and instead submit ourselves to God's truth. And by forgiving our spouses, we create the opportunity for them to recognize and receive God's invitation to be reshaped by His grace.

When we come to God in repentance, His response isn't, "I'm God, and I know you're just going to do this again in two weeks." He simply says, "I forgive you," and offers us the empowerment to change. God doesn't speak failure into our futures; He declares hope and promise over every struggle. Let us do likewise for each other.

Opening Your Spirit

Offense causes us to close our spirits. In our efforts not to get hurt again, we build walls around our hearts. We may think these walls protect us, but in reality they obstruct our ability to receive and give Christ's love. Without His love, our lives will be devoid of purpose and power. Our goal will be self-preservation, and our actions will exude selfishness. Eventually, our hearts will become like stone and our lives will be marked by indifference toward others. This is the antithesis of the gospel message.

You may recognize the names of the Sea of Galilee and the Dead Sea. These are two of the largest and most well-known bodies of water in Israel. The Sea of Galilee receives water from the north and releases it to the south. This constant flow makes the Sea of Galilee conducive to life, and various aquatic inhabitants flourish within its depths. The Dead Sea, by contrast, only takes in water. Everything it receives, it retains. Because the Dead Sea has no outlet, nothing more than tiny bacteria or fungi can survive in its salty ecosystem—hence its name.

When we retain offense, we become like the Dead Sea. Our closed spirits cause our marriages to become environments where no good thing can flourish or even survive. Through forgiveness, we reopen our hearts so God's power can flow in and through us.

A refusal to give and receive forgiveness inevitably leads to the poisoning of the soul. We are not self-sufficient. Only God is. Our vitality requires a harmonious exchange with those we do life with; we must freely give and receive.

The Limits of Forgiveness

You may be thinking, *I feel like my spouse constantly needs to be forgiven. My forgiveness is not inexhaustible. There has to be a limit!* The disciples thought similarly:

> Then Peter came to [Jesus] and asked, "Lord, how often should I forgive someone who sins against me? Seven times?"

> "No, not seven times," Jesus replied, "but seventy times seven!" (Matthew 18:21-22)

When Peter asked this question, he was trying to be as magnanimous as possible. Peter grew up under the Law, which said, "You must show no pity for the guilty! Your rule should be life for life, eye for eye, tooth for tooth, hand for hand, foot for foot" (Deuteronomy 19:21). So when Peter offered to forgive up to seven times, he expected Jesus to say, "Yes, Peter, you've got it!"

We know from elsewhere in the New Testament that Peter's offer of seven pardons was the number of times he thought he might need to forgive someone in a day (see Luke 17:3-4). So Jesus' response—to forgive "seventy times seven"—was not merely His mandating a greater limit of forgiveness for a lifetime of offenses. He was communicating to Peter that forgiveness should be given without measure.

For someone to sin at the level Jesus described, they would have to commit 490 offenses in one day! To sin that profusely, your spouse would have to offend you once every three minutes—provided neither of you went to sleep. That's a lot of sinning, more than anyone is likely to achieve. But even if your spouse could sin against you more than 490 times in one day, that doesn't mean you can stop forgiving them after offense 490.

In Scripture, the number seven symbolizes completeness, specifically between earth and heaven. Jesus used the number 490, a multiple of seven, to convey that we are to forgive completely, following the standard of our heavenly Father. This generous forgiveness is only possible because we have been restored to God through Christ. In Him, there is harmony between the Father and His children. We are therefore empowered to forgive because we are new creations with new hearts. Our hearts have freely received His forgiveness, and in order to remain spiritually healthy, we must freely offer forgiveness to others.

We know Jesus wants our forgiveness to be inexhaustible because after His conversation with Peter, He told a parable about a forgiving king and an unforgiving servant, which concluded with this explanation:

> "Then the angry king sent the man to prison to be tortured until he had paid his entire debt.

> "That's what my heavenly Father will do to you if you refuse to forgive your brothers and sisters from your heart." (Matthew 18:34-35)

We will not receive forgiveness if we refuse to forgive. There are no exceptions. Why is it so important to God that we forgive? Because in forgiveness we discover and imitate His nature. We transcend the limitations of our inherent human wretchedness and instead conform to the likeness of our Father. In God's forgiveness we are made whole, and we are invited—even charged—to extend His wholeness to those whom we forgive. If your spouse is frequently asking for forgiveness, then God has blessed you with the opportunity to be an agent of His healing power.

For more on the topic of offense, see John's book The Bait of Satan.

Day 3

The Fight: John's Story

There was a time in our marriage when we were offended with each other for about eighteen months straight. The same argument resurfaced over and over again. We even made subtle jabs at each other in front of our children. The older ones were not oblivious to what was happening, and they would make comments like, "Can you please not talk about this during dinner?" Our pain and disunity were a source of constant tension in our household, and they were eating away at our marriage and family.

One night, after we berated each other in our usual fashion, I (John) stormed out of the house. I was furious with Lisa, and I immediately started complaining to God. I lamented Lisa's shortcomings and shortsightedness. I felt like God had stuck me with a wife who was unsupportive and unnecessarily critical. How, I wondered, could I continue in life with a wife like this?

I'll never forget how God responded. The Holy Spirit didn't say a word to me about how sorry He felt for me, nor did He address the pain I was in; rather He simply whispered to me, "Son, I want you to think of one thing you appreciate about Lisa and then thank Me for it."

It took me a while to respond, but I finally mumbled, "She's a good mom." As the words escaped my mouth, I felt a stirring of life in my soul. God prompted me to continue. I said, "Lord, thank You that Lisa's a really good cook." Then, "Thank You that she's beautiful." More words began to flow, and I proceeded to gratefully list Lisa's good qualities at the rate of a machine gun.

At that point I was no longer upset with Lisa; I was upset with myself. I thought, *You're a complete idiot! Your wife is amazing, and you've been a jerk to her. What is wrong with you?* I became painfully aware of how horribly I had treated Lisa. She was my chosen wife and the mother of our children, an absolute blessing from God, and I had treated her like an inconvenience to my calling.

When I left the house, Lisa was fed up with me and I with her. But now I just wanted to go and tell her how grateful I was for her. As I rushed home, I thought to myself, *I may not be well-received, but I just have to tell her how grateful I am for her.*

Once I arrived at the house, I found Lisa and exclaimed, "Lisa, I am so sorry! I've been such a jerk. Please forgive me. You are an amazing mother and excellent wife, and you are the desire of my heart." I shared what God had brought to my remembrance, then started praising her for all her magnificent traits, qualities, and gifts. The words poured out of my heart like a river.

As I spoke, Lisa softened and began to cry. Unbeknownst to me, while I was gone, she had prayed, "God, if you bring John back and he tells me he's sorry, I'm going to open my heart again."

The Fight: Lisa's Story

Things had gotten so bad during those eighteen months that I stopped wearing my engagement ring. I would tell John that we were married but not engaged, whatever that meant. I started to believe that I had no love for John. My refusal to forgive had caused my heart to grow cold, and our relationship was in great peril.

At the time, John was traveling a lot, and I began to enjoy his time away more than I enjoyed him being home. *Life is easier when he is gone,* I thought. *He just makes me crazy when he's at home—all that fighting and tension.*

Desperate, I began to cry out to the Lord, "God, we are at a standstill. John is not being nice at all! Father, I know You must be upset by his behavior!"

On and on I went; almost daily I made my case before the Father. But when I was finally quiet, I heard Him speak. "Lisa, tell Me I'm enough for you."

At first I was a bit frightened. If I said God was enough, did that mean John wasn't going to change? I echoed back the words: "Father, You're enough for me."

Then I found myself repeating the question. "But what about John?"

Again I heard, "Tell Me I am enough for you."

"You're enough for me."[5]

Those words became my refrain. Every time conflict or disappointment arose, I prayed, "Jesus, You're enough for me." Over time, the revelation took root in my heart and my prayers transformed. What started as a broken confession ("Jesus, You're enough for me") became an overflow of satisfaction in God: "Jesus, You're more than enough for me!"

Soon God had done His work in both our hearts. John came home from a trip, and I gladly picked him up from the airport (a task I had allowed others to handle during the months when I preferred he not come home at all). I was happy to greet my husband, and I found he had brought me a beautiful gift.

That moment marked a new beginning for our marriage. It is interesting that even before the change happened, God opened up both of our hearts through gratitude.

In marriage, if we commit to imitating Jesus' example of forgiving even when mistreated, we will see our unions stay healthy and even flourish. Unbeknownst to us at the time, one of the greatest examples we gave our children was saying we were sorry to one another and then forgiving each other. Our children came to understand that we are imperfect inhabitants dwelling in an imperfect world, but God's perfect forgiveness in our hearts can cover a multitude of sins. Those sins, designed to wreak havoc and destroy our union, actually ended up becoming life lessons to our children of the love, grace, and forgiveness of God. We saw these words of wisdom fulfilled in our family:

Love prospers when a fault is forgiven.... (Proverbs 17:9)

If you choose to hold on to offense, everyone loses because love dwindles. However, when you choose to forgive, everyone in your family wins because love flourishes.

Fear

The next thing to be addressed in your relationship is fear. For the first ten years of our marriage, I (Lisa) struggled with the fear of abandonment. My father and my first pastor had both left their wives for younger women. Because of what I had experienced, I allowed fearful thoughts to linger unchecked in my mind. They didn't yell; they whispered, *Eventually all men leave. Don't let them get too close. Then they can't disappoint you.* This kind of thinking caused me to even resist small displays of affection. When John hugged me, it wasn't long before I'd start patting him so I could pull away.

One day, after one of my "pat-and-pull-aways," John asked me point blank, "How old will we have to be before you realize I'm not going to leave you? Are you going to wait until we're seventy?" I was stunned.

"I'll wait as long as it takes," he continued, "but we're going to miss out on a lot of fun in the meantime."

I realized I was making John pay for the disappointments I had with other men. I thought, *Why should John have to pay for their shortcomings? That's not fair. In an effort to protect myself, I am sabotaging our relationship.* My fear of losing John in the future was robbing both of us in the present. I decided then that I would rather love John completely, even at the risk of losing him, than love him halfway and look back with regret on what might have been.

Fear and distrust keep us from thriving in marriage, for fear tenaciously clings to the past while refusing to believe something better can arise in the future. If we want God to do a new thing in our marriages, we must choose to abandon fear and accept what love would forecast for our futures. Fear expects failure, while love ultimately can never fail.

Fear is a spiritual force in direct opposition to God's love and protection in our lives. It is the opposite of love, for both love and fear operate from belief in the unseen. Love challenges us to doubt what we see and believe for what we cannot. Fear urges us to believe what is seen and doubt the unseen. When faced with the fear of failure or the hope of love, we can choose to believe one or the other but not both. Fear displaces love; love casts out fear.[6]

...Perfect love expels all fear. If we are afraid, it is for fear of punishment, and this shows that we have not fully experienced his perfect love. We love each other because he loved us first. (1 John 4:18-19)

Love's ability to transform is greater than fear's ability to ensnare. The perfect love that expels fear is only found in the experience of God's love. Through the power of His love, we can forsake concern for self, because we know that God will faithfully tend to our needs. But if we don't spend time in God's presence, we cannot have an intimate knowledge of His loving nature; for His faithfulness manifests in His presence.

Without knowledge of God's true nature, we will live in constant fear of abandonment by Him or by our spouses, which is a twisted form of punishment. As we grow more and more secure in God's love for us, we can become free from fear and offer selfless love to our spouses. God's Word says:

...Let us continue to love one another, for love comes from God. Anyone who loves is a child of God and knows God. But anyone who does not love does not know God, for God is love. (1 John 4:7-8)

The stronghold of fear is what causes us to say things like, "If my spouse ever cheats on me, I will never forgive him." Such vows, which are intended to shield us in the future, keep us from embracing the power of God's love today. We must learn to trust God to care for our hearts, even if a spouse wounds, rejects, or betrays us. God has asked us to surrender our fears to Him. Refusal to do so tells God we don't believe He is capable of directing our lives. We cannot submit to Jesus' lordship without surrendering our fears to Him.

Day 4

Family Curses

As we began our marriage, we knew God wanted to do something new in us and our children. But there were obvious strongholds among our parents and grandparents: things like alcoholism, immorality, and witchcraft had plagued our family lines. Before we could receive a new legacy, we had to confront the curses that had plagued our families for generations. These things could only be combatted in prayer and dismantled by the Word of God.

The specifics of family curses look different for each couple, but here is one example. In a previous chapter, we mentioned that our family backgrounds are quite different. I (Lisa) was concerned about how John's family would react to the blatant dysfunction in mine. At our engagement dinner, my father was drunk and shamelessly flirted with John's mother—right in front of her husband! His actions were focused on hurting my mother rather than on any real intentions toward John's mom. Later, John's mother expressed her deep concern that our marriage would be the first time anyone with divorce in their background had joined their pristine clan. I overheard her say, "We've never had divorce in our family before."

I thought, *Is that how she sees me? Am I going to mess up this lineage?*

I left the dinner feeling both my mother's hurt and so much of my own shame. It seemed if there were scales that could weigh the premarital "good" and "bad" of family contribution, the good was drastically tipped in John's favor. I was bringing in all the bad: adultery, divorce, and addiction were among the issues in my family line.

Breakthrough came when I realized God wasn't concerned about John's good or my bad. He wanted a holy lineage.

Listen to me, O royal daughter; take to heart what I say. Forget your people and your family far away. For your royal husband delights in your beauty; honor him, for he is your lord. ...Your sons will become kings like their father. You will make them rulers over many lands. I will bring honor to your name in every generation. Therefore, the nations will praise you forever and ever. (Psalm 45:10-12, 16-17)

This passage is primarily a description of Jesus and His Bride, but God used it to paint a picture of His promise for my life, a promise not limited by the mistakes in my family's past. When I read the words *O royal daughter*, something in me came alive. God was speaking to *me* as His royal daughter. In that moment, a new understanding of my identity in Christ was revealed. I rejected the strongholds of my past and embraced a new hope for my family's future.

I realized that instead of the likeness of my natural father (an adulterer, alcoholic, and profoundly broken man), my children would inherit not only the likeness of their earthly father (a godly man), but even more, they would inherit the likeness of their Lord. I stood on the promise that my sons would become princes of the Most High.

As we addressed our family curses, we saw the Word of God proved true. Our family has flourished in the promises God established over our lives during those times of prayer and declaration.

Prayer to Break Family Curses

Galatians 3:13 says, "Christ redeemed us from the curse of the law by becoming a curse for us" (ESV). Whatever curses have followed your family through the generations, in Christ, you are no longer subject to them.

If you are aware of curses in your family line, we want to position you to break off what has limited and defined your legacy. This prayer will help you address Satan's strongholds with the sword of God's Word. Freedom from family curses doesn't happen by accident; you must identify and attack Satan's schemes. His goal is to keep you from enjoying the joy, peace, and fulfillment that God has set before you. But through the authority you now possess in Christ, you can see your enemy vanquished.

Please take a moment to pause and set time apart before proceeding with this prayer. If you plan to pray right now, please make sure you are alone or with only your spouse or a close friend or prayer partner. This is a private and personal time, and you will need to speak out loud your petitions, renouncements, and response.

The prayer below addresses some of the specific curses that threatened our marriage and family. We have constructed this prayer by combining scriptures, for the Word is the sharp and powerful, two-edged Sword of the Spirit. If there are issues in your family line not covered by this prayer, we encourage you to find scriptures that address those issues with God's truth and promise. Craft a bold declaration in agreement with God's Word and break the curses off your life by the power of Jesus' name. We have included references for your further study at the close of the prayer.

Dear heavenly Father,

I come before You in the name of Your precious Son, Jesus; I enter Your gates with thanksgiving and come into Your courts with praise. I am overwhelmed by Your gracious mercy and love for me, and I thank You in advance for the mighty work of redemption You have wrought in my life.

Now I intend to make a covenant with the LORD, the God of Israel. You are the LORD, the God of heaven and earth, the great and awesome God, who keeps His covenant of love with those who love Him and obey His commands. Let Your ear be attentive and Your eyes open to hear the prayer of Your servant. I confess my sins and the sins of my father's house, every transgression we have committed against You. Forgive us, for we have acted very wickedly toward You. We have been covered with shame because we sinned against You. But You, Lord, our God, are merciful and forgiving, even though we have rebelled against You and have not obeyed the LORD our God or kept the laws He gave us through His servants, the prophets. We ask You to circumcise our hearts and roll away the sin, shame, and reproach of our pasts.

I confess and renounce my sin and the sins of my forefathers, for any and all involvement in the occult, witchcraft, or divination. (Pause here, and stay sensitive to add anything the Holy Spirit brings to your attention to specifically renounce before continuing. This may include, but certainly is not limited to, astrology, séances, horror movies, games, books, etc.) *I renounce my involvement in these things and break their curse off my life and off the lives of my children, their children, and their children's children.*

I confess and renounce my sin and/or the sins of my forefathers in the area of drug and alcohol abuse. Father, close any door this may have opened in the spirit realm to sin, bondage, or oppression. I renounce my involvement with (specifically call the drugs out by name, if applicable), *and I break the power of their curse off my life and off the lives of my children, their children, and their children's children. In Jesus' name, amen.*

We will continue to build on this principle by addressing curses and soul ties related to sexual sin in a later chapter. Because of the finality of Jesus' victory on the cross, you are free from these curses. You need not fear them nor worry that these sins will follow you or your children. You have established a new legacy for your family today.

For further study, see: Psalm 100:4; 2 Chronicles 29:10-11; Nehemiah 1:5-7; Daniel 9:8-10; Joshua 5:9; Matthew 10:34; Hebrews 4:12; 2 Chronicles 29:5-6.[7]

Day 5

Controlling In-Laws

The issue of controlling in-laws is more common among newlyweds, but it can certainly be a factor beyond the early days of marriage. When we face conflict between our spouses and our families, it's natural to want to defend the parents (or other relations) we've known all our lives. All of us should have great love and respect for our parents. But while you may often welcome your parents' counsel, once you are married, your first obligation is to your spouse.

Before our oldest son got married, I (John) told him, "Addison, I will not tell you what to do in any area unless you ask for my advice. I will no longer initiate direction for your life. You are establishing your own household, and I want to give you space to learn and grow." Addison has expressed his gratitude for this stance and approaches me whenever he desires my counsel.

My desire is not to control my son or mold him into a mini me. I want Addison to become everything God created him to be, and too much of my involvement in his marriage could keep him from assuming his role as leader of his home. (Frankly, I have been amazed by what he's done with his household. It's much better than what I had accomplished when I was his age!)

Scripture is clear:

…A man *leaves* his father and mother and is joined to his wife, and the two are united into one. (Genesis 2:24, emphasis added)

To *leave* your father and mother in this manner means leaving the authority of your parent's household. It also means you leave any unhealthy influence your parents have over you. It's important to honor your parents, but you can honor them without obeying them. You have formed a new household with a new hierarchy. Your parents are no longer your authority figures, so they should not direct your life or marriage.

You may have to deal with in-laws who try to get too involved in your marriage. Early on, one of our in-laws tried to manipulate us and bring division to our union. Her involvement was becoming destructive, and our subtle attempts to address the issue were to no avail. Finally, we met with this individual (whom we both honor and love) and expressed our position clearly.

I (John) said, "You are not going to be involved in running my household. This is a brand-new home. We honor you, but you will not control the decisions in this house. You will not manipulate to get your way." I had to use strong words because more indirect approaches had failed. Thankfully, this relative realized what was happening, and now she holds a proper, healthy place in our relationship.

As couples, we must guard our unions against every form of attack, including those from our family members. Often these attacks aren't malicious and can seem innocuous. They frequently take the form of derogatory jests, but such subtle remarks are always destructive. When I conduct marriage ceremonies, I look at all the friends and family in attendance and say, "Woe to you who speaks against this union. This is a union ordained by God. Don't you dare attempt to manipulate or separate it. Speak only life over what God has established today."

When Addison got married, we intentionally resolved not to make him choose between his wife, Juli, and us. The truth is, he made his choice the day he married Juli, and we're thrilled with his decision! In this context of family dynamics, love never makes people choose. Love supports and builds bridges between old and new relationships. We love Juli and feel she is much more a daughter than a daughter-in-law. This closeness is only possible because we have respected her new household and allowed her and Addison to write their own story.

Unrealistic Expectations

Unrealistic expectations are among the top-cited reasons for divorce in the United States.[8] Many of us enter marriage expecting perpetual bliss, nonstop sex, and relational ease. We don't expect marriage to faithfully and relentlessly expose our selfishness and insecurities, nor do we anticipate the weaknesses and faults we'll encounter in our spouses. Our misguided expectations can become a source of bitterness and discontentment, which will invariably keep us from building godly unions.

Unrealistic expectations are often fueled by unwise comparison. We are steeped in a culture oriented toward entertainment. We're therefore constantly provided with opportunities to compare our marriages to those depicted on the screen. Movies and television offer us love without work, beauty without sacrifice, and trust without risk. They highlight romantic facets of relationship without portraying the less "Hollywood" moments of life.

If you've been married for any length of time, you've realized marriage is made of more than romantic dates, seamless compatibility, and days free from responsibility. Marriage is hard work, and it's often messy.

Just because your marriage is hard doesn't mean that you shouldn't be married. Challenges in marriage are good because they stretch you. They refine your character and increase your capacity. This relationship is about *largeness*, remember? Everyone loves the idea of growing and maturing until they encounter something that requires maturation.

The issue of unrealistic expectations isn't only about media portrayals of marriage. We also make the mistake of comparing our marriages with those of our friends or neighbors. This is a horrible idea. There is no way for us to know what's going on behind the scenes of their relationships. Everything may appear fine and dandy, but they may be destroying each other behind closed doors.

It is also tempting to compare seasons within our relationships. Maybe we compare a current season—one with kids, diapers, and little free time—to what our relationship was like before we had children. Logically, this doesn't make any sense. There is no way your life can stay exactly the same after you have kids. Parenting involves a lot less freedom and a lot more responsibility. Having children inherently changes your life, so your marriage relationship will look different too. We know this isn't rocket science, but how often do we find ourselves making foolish comparisons that belittle or strain the joy and fulfillment available in the present?

Theodore Roosevelt said, "Comparison is the thief of joy." If you are going to find joy in your marriage, you must stop comparing your relationship with ones that seem better, whether the other relationships are those of your neighbors or the ones depicted on a screen. You will never find joy in comparison. Joy is not petty and therefore cannot be obtained through pettiness. It transcends circumstances, is not confined to feelings, and finds its strength in an awareness of the big picture—the totality of God's plan for your life.

Joy is a fruit of the Spirit (see Galatians 5:22-23), which means it is received from God and not from circumstances. It cannot be generated by human will. While happiness is a feeling affected by temporal struggles, joy transcends difficulties. It stems from the hope inspired by our position in Christ. If we lack joy in God, we'll lack the strength we need to do marriage well, because His joy is our strength (see Nehemiah 8:10). Paul echoed this sentiment in his words to the church in Philippi:

> Rejoice in the Lord always; again I will say, rejoice. Let your reasonableness be known to everyone. The Lord is at hand; do not be anxious about anything, but in everything by prayer and supplication with thanksgiving let your requests be made known to God. And the peace of God, which surpasses all understanding, will guard your hearts and your minds in Christ Jesus. (Philippians 4:4-7 ESV)

When you find yourself anxious about your relationship, bring your requests to God with joyful thanks. He has promised to trade your worries for His peace. That's a good exchange!

Unrealistic expectations will steal your joy and therefore rob you of strength for your marriage. Do not fall prey to this trap. Identify any expectations that have created a stronghold in your relationship and repent for allowing them to take precedence over the truth of God's Word and His unique plan for your life.

Your Turn

Please take some time to talk with your spouse about the content covered in this chapter. Ask the Holy Spirit to guide you as you write down what needs to be cleared away in your marriage. Some of the necessary alterations will be attitude adjustments and behavioral changes, which God will enable by the power of His grace. Others, like generational curses, must be confronted in prayer.

Don't be discouraged if you find your list fills several pages. This exercise is not about how much is "wrong" in the present, nor is it about which party in your marriage has the most problems. It is about the magnificent things that can be brought forth in your future. By addressing these issues now, you are positioning your family to write a brilliant story, a legacy of heaven revealed on earth. We want you to clear the decks so that you can move forward free of everything that would obstruct you from receiving all God has for you. We've constructed the prayer below to start you on your way.

May this be a sacred moment.

Father, we thank You for offering us a new start and a new legacy. As we make record of the things that need to be cleared from our relationship, we pray for an atmosphere of heaven to surround us.

We ask You, Holy Spirit, to lead and instruct us.

We pray that the angels of God will encamp around us, ready to execute vengeance upon the enemy who has plagued our families from generation to generation.

We pray for great grace to empower forgiveness and transformation.

We pray for the renewing of our minds according to Your Word.

We ask for a revelation of Your love that will cast out every fear.

We ask for restoration of trust and refinement of relationships.

We pray for You to bring unity where there has been division.

We ask that You inspire us to dream according to Your promises, not according to any ungodly expectation.

We speak freedom over our household. We speak freedom into our marriage and into our individual lives, in the name of Jesus Christ. We declare that the kingdom of God has come within us. The will of God shall be done in our marriage and home, on earth as it is in heaven. In Jesus' mighty name, amen.

FAMILY CHECKUP

Test yourselves to make sure you are solid in the faith. Don't drift along taking everything for granted. Give yourselves regular checkups. You need firsthand evidence, not mere hearsay, that Jesus Christ is in you. Test it out. If you fail the test, do something about it.

—2 Corinthians 13:5 The Message

In order to move forward, it is sometimes helpful to look back and understand how you got where you are. This family checkup will help you assess and address the clutter that needs to be cleared from the decks of your marriage. Take a few moments to stop, think, and answer honestly.

Think back to your childhood. How would you describe the overall atmosphere of your home?

_____

_____

Examples: peaceful, chaotic, loving, unloving, open, closed, generous, stingy, fearful, wonderful, warm and welcoming or cold and hostile.

Briefly describe your parents' overall relationship (communication, affection, friendship, etc.).

_____

_____

How did your parents work through disagreements and conflicts? How did they treat each other?

_____

_____

When you messed up or misbehaved, how were you corrected? After the correction, was your offense held against you for a little while, or were you fully restored and shown love?

_____

_____

COMPLETE THESE SENTENCES:

"The things I **enjoyed** about growing up and want to duplicate in my home are..."

_____

_____

"The things I **disliked** and don't want to repeat in my marriage and family are..."

_____

_____

Review your answers and compare them to your current marriage and home life. What *similarities* do you see in your home's atmosphere, your relationship with your spouse, how you work through conflict, and how you discipline your kids? See any connections?

_____

_____

_____

Based on this inventory, what do you and your mate need to clear from the decks of your marriage?

_____

_____

_____

Share your answers with your spouse. Pray and surrender what needs to be cleared by the Holy Spirit.

GIVING ALLOWANCE

*Make **allowance** for each other's faults, and forgive anyone who offends you. Remember, the Lord forgave you, so you must forgive others.*

—Colossians 3:13

Do you give your spouse *allowance*? No, not money. We're talking about space to make mistakes—room to grow into God's image by His grace. The fact is, we all need allowance because we all have faults. When we forgive, we imitate our heavenly Father, becoming conduits of His grace who empower our spouses to change. In the words of author **C.S. Lewis**,

"To be a Christian means to forgive the inexcusable, because God has forgiven the inexcusable in you. This is hard. It is perhaps not so hard to forgive a single injury. But to forgive the incessant provocations of daily life—to keep on forgiving the bossy mother-in-law, the bullying husband, the nagging wife, the selfish daughter, the deceitful son—how can we do it? Only, I think, by remembering where we stand, by meaning our words when we say in our prayers each night, 'Forgive us our trespasses *as we forgive those who trespass against us.*' We are offered forgiveness on no other terms. To refuse it means to refuse God's mercy for ourselves. There is no hint of exceptions and God means what He says."[9]

In what areas do you need your spouse to give you allowance? Where do you need space to make mistakes and grow in godly character? Name three areas you're aware of and working on.

_____

_____

_____

_____

_____

Name three areas in which your spouse needs allowance from you. Are you providing it? If not, why?

What does God say will happen if you choose to hold on to offense toward your mate? Carefully read Matthew 6:14-15; 18:21-35; Mark 11:25 and write what the Holy Spirit reveals.

God's forgiveness is *limitless*! If you're having a hard time forgiving your spouse, take time to look back over your life. In what ways have you offended the Lord in your thoughts, words, and actions? As you remember the depth of your own sin and the excruciating pain Jesus suffered to pay for it, the Holy Spirit will soften your heart and give you grace to forgive.

A PRAYER OF REPENTANCE AND RELEASE

"Lord, forgive me for holding onto offense against my spouse. I no longer want to keep a record of their wrongs. You forgive me of my sins and never bring them up again. Give me the power and desire to do the same. I release my mate into Your hands. Pour Your love and grace into our hearts. Help me to genuinely love and forgive them and to give them allowance to make mistakes and grow. I bless them with health, wisdom, peace, joy, love, favor, confidence, revelation of Your Word, and an awesome, intimate relationship with You. Thank You, Father, for healing our marriage. In Jesus' name, amen."

Allow the Holy Spirit to work His loving, forgiving nature into you through time in His presence and by carefully meditating on passages like these: 1 Corinthians 13; Romans 5:5; Ephesians 3:16-19; 1 Peter 3:8-9.

IT'S ALL ABOUT PERSPECTIVE

*...**Fix your thoughts** on what is true and good and right. Think about things that are pure and lovely, and dwell on the fine, good things in others. Think about all you can praise God for and be glad about.*

—Philippians 4:8 TLB

When it comes to thinking about your mate, what are you focused on? If you fix your thoughts on your spouse's faults and failures, the problems in your marriage will be magnified. On the other hand, if you fix your thoughts on things you can be thankful for, you'll see your relationship in a whole new light! Your marriage, like all of life, is all about perspective.

The lens through which you view your mate will directly affect your relationship. Overall, how do you treat your mate? Reflect on the kinds of words, actions, and attitudes you typically display.

_____

_____

_____

_____

Pray and ask the Lord to reveal the truth of your treatment. What's He showing you? What is He asking you to change with His help?

Want a new perspective of your spouse's value? Carefully meditate on Philippians 4:8. Then make a list of the *top ten* things (traits, qualities, gifts) about him or her you can thank God for.

_____

_____

_____

_____

_____

Continue to reflect on and add to this list over the next thirty days. Be intentional to sincerely express your gratitude for these qualities to your spouse, too!

Fear distorts our vision. It keeps us focused on what seems wrong in our spouses, ourselves, and our situations. In many ways, *fear* is **F**alse **E**vidence **A**ppearing **R**eal. What are your greatest fears regarding your relationship with your spouse? Ask the Lord to reveal them.

_____

_____

_____

_____

Run these fears through the filter of Philippians 4:8. Are they true, good, or right? Are they pure and lovely? Can you praise God for them? Anything that fails to pass this test must be thrown out and replaced with truth.

Many times our fears in the present are birthed out of disappointments and hurts from the past. Afraid of being hurt again, we unknowingly attempt to make our spouses pay the price for the shortcomings of our parents, previous boyfriends/girlfriends, or former spouses.

Pause and pray, "Holy Spirit, how did these fears form? On what are they based? How can I trust You more and see them eradicated from my life?" Be still and listen. What is He revealing?

_____

_____

_____

_____

FREEDOM FROM FAMILY CURSES

Christ paid the price to free us from the curse...
by becoming cursed instead of us....

—Galatians 3:13 GW

God wants to do something brand new in your family! He says, "Behold, I am doing a new thing; now it springs forth, do you not perceive it? I will make a way in the wilderness and rivers in the desert" (Isaiah 43:19 ESV). As **Joyce Meyer** shares:

"Jesus came to open the prison doors and set the captives free. ...You may have had a miserable past, you may even be in current circumstances that are very negative and depressing. You may be facing situations that are so bad it seems you have no real reason to hope. But I say to you boldly, *your future is not determined by your past or your present!* Get a new mind-set. Believe that with God all things are possible (Luke 18:27)."[10]

Christ has paid the price to set you, your spouse, and your children free from every curse that has been lurking in your bloodline. All you need to do is *enforce* His victory. Get quiet before the Lord and pray, "Holy Spirit, what curses of ungodly behavior are operating in my bloodline? My spouse's? Please show us so we can address them and experience true freedom."

_____

_____

_____

_____

Once the Holy Spirit reveals the curses, surrender them to Him. Refer to the prayer provided in the chapter and trust Him to bring breakthrough.

Sometimes we unknowingly perpetuate problems that plague our families by making vows (or promises) to ourselves. When vows are spoken, walls are erected around our hearts. These vows are meant to protect us from further hurt, but instead they imprison and cause greater pain.

You are trapped by the words of your own mouth, caught by your own promise.

—Proverbs 6:2 GW

Pause and pray, "Holy Spirit, have I made any vows to myself? If so, what are they?" Be still and listen. Repent of any vows He reveals and ask Him to set you free from all fears, in Jesus' name.

_____

_____

_____

*We speak vows out of fear. Afraid of being hurt again, we often say things like, "**I will never** allow a man/woman to.... **If my husband/wife ever** (cheats on me, hits me, etc.), I will..." If you have spoken such vows internally or aloud, repent. Ask the Lord to help you trust Him to defend and protect you.*

No weapon that is formed against you shall prosper, and every tongue that shall rise against you in judgment you shall show to be in the wrong. This [peace, righteousness, security, triumph over opposition] is the *heritage* of the servants of the Lord [those in whom the ideal Servant of the Lord is reproduced]....

—Isaiah 54:17 AMP, emphasis added

Through your relationship with Jesus, you are freed from every curse and inherit every spiritual blessing (see Ephesians 1:3). Carefully read these scriptures and identify some of the blessings available to you and your family in Christ: Matthew 11:28; 16:19; Luke 10:19; 11:13; John 4:14; 7:38-39; 14:27; 15:11; 1 Corinthians 1:30; 2 Corinthians 5:21; 2 Peter 1:3-4. What else is the Holy Spirit revealing in these verses?

_____

_____

_____

_____

MANAGING EXPECTATIONS

*...[God] Himself has said, I will not in any way fail you nor give you up
nor leave you without support. [I will] not, [I will] not, [I will] not
in any degree leave you helpless nor forsake nor let [you]
down (relax My hold on you)! [Assuredly not!]*

—Hebrews 13:5 AMP

Expectation. It's "a strong belief that something will happen or be the case in the future."[11] When we have expectations of people, we have strong feelings or beliefs about how successful or good they will be, particularly in relation to us. We generally have the greatest expectations of those we're closest to, especially our spouses. Author and speaker **Patrick M. Morley** explains:

> "All of us bring expectations into marriage—different, often unrealistic expectations. Those expectations are based on (1) our image of marriage and (2) our unmet needs. We each have an image of what the ideal marriage looks like in our minds. We may have gained that image from our parents—what they said and did, family folklore about our ancestors, a friend's parents, watching television, reading books, movie stars, or a hero."[12]

Unrealistic expectations can exist in any area of your marriage. Money matters, communication, household chores, raising children, relationships with friends, sex—you name it. Pause and pray, "Lord, do I have any unrealistic expectations of my marriage? If so, what are they?"

What is the Holy Spirit showing you? Write it down, along with any actions He is prompting you to take.

How can you change unrealistic expectations into realistic ones? **Patrick Morley** continues:

"We must learn to *give without expecting anything* in return. We must learn to *communicate our expectations* to our mates, then listen to see if they agree we are being realistic."[13]

Ask your spouse, "Do you feel I have any unrealistic expectations of you? If so, what are they?" Be respectful and listen without interrupting. Write what they share.

_____

_____

_____

_____

If you have had unrealistic expectations of your mate, take time to sincerely apologize for putting pressure on them. Pray and ask the Lord to bring healing to your marriage and to cultivate realistic expectations in you both.

Ultimately, our expectations should be in God and what He promises in His Word. He is faithful and will not fail! Pray, "Lord, am I putting any expectations on my spouse to meet needs only You can fill? If so, please show me. Give me the grace to trust You to meet these needs." Be still and listen. What is the Holy Spirit showing you?

_____

_____

_____

_____

DISCUSSION QUESTIONS

If you are using this book as part of the Messenger Series on
The Story of Marriage, *please refer to video session 3.*

1 | Disagreements in marriage are inevitable, but how we deal with them makes all the difference. Think about it. Husband and wife are two different people in the process of becoming one. Each is entirely unique. Consequently, each spouse thinks, processes, and emotes differently. The ways spouses see a situation, a person, an opportunity, etc., will be different. Have you ever thought about this? How does understanding your spouse's uniqueness help you appreciate them and see them in a positive new light?

2 | Through Christ, forgiveness is available to all who ask. But what if you asked God to forgive you for something and He said, "I don't know if I want to forgive you. You're probably just going to do it again. I want to see some change first"? How would this response make you feel? Have you ever said or thought this when your spouse asked for forgiveness? How might this make them feel?

3 | God's forgiveness is not a reward for modified behavior. It is His vote of confidence. Stop and think: How do God's unconditional love and forgiveness empower and motivate you to change? In light of this, what attitude should you adopt toward your spouse regarding forgiveness? What will this do for them?

"Forgiveness is the only way to break the cycle of blame—and pain—
in a relationship... It does not settle all questions of blame and
justice and fairness... But it does allow relationships to start over."

—Philip Yancey[14]

4 | Fear is a spiritual force that is in direct opposition to God's love and protection in our lives. If not identified and addressed, fear will paralyze us from growing into the largeness of marriage. Husbands, what are some fears men face in their relationships with their wives? Wives, what are some fears women face in their relationships with their husbands? What specific ways have you found to overcome these?

FEARS HUSBANDS FACE   **FEARS WIVES FACE**

_____   _____

_____   _____

_____   _____

_____   _____

_____   _____

5 | Unrealistic expectations in marriage are a breeding ground for offense, frustration, and disappointment. The enemy cunningly employs entertainment and media to produce and feed impractical views of our spouses and to sow seeds of dissatisfaction. Stop and think. How do movies, music, television shows, magazines, books, and the Internet affect and infect our perspectives on our mates and our marriages? What practical steps can we take to guard our hearts and minds against unrealistic expectations?

Leader: Share Philippians 4:8 as a litmus test for our media choices.

> _For as he thinks in his heart, so is he…._
>
> —Proverbs 23:7 NKJV

6 | Have you encountered difficult situations with controlling in-laws? Without giving any names, share about one of them. If you were able to overcome the challenge, explain how God helped you to do so. If you are still dealing with it, ask your group to pray for God's grace to empower you to handle it properly.

CHAPTER SUMMARY:

- Clearing the decks of your marriage will position you to move into the largeness God intended.

- Forgiveness is an act of liberation for both the offender and the offended. By God's grace, we can freely and without measure forgive others and receive His forgiveness.

- We cannot change our spouses; only God can. But we can work with Him and allow Him to change us.

- An attitude of gratitude for your spouse will open your heart to love, forgive, and extend God's grace to them so they—and you—can grow and change.

- When you choose to forgive, everyone in your family wins because love causes us to flourish.

- Experiencing God's love exposes and expels fear from our lives. Allowing His love to work in and through us helps destroy fear in our mate and covers our faults and failures.

- Before you can build a new legacy, you must confront the curses that have plagued your family. Through the completed work of Christ, every curse is crushed!

- Whatever the condition of your marriage, God can change it because He is in it. Nothing is impossible with Him!

FOUR

Rise and Build

*...“You know that the rulers in this world lord it over their people,
and officials flaunt their authority over those under them. But among you
it will be different. Whoever wants to be a leader among you must be
your servant, and whoever wants to be first among you must become
your slave. For even the Son of Man came not to be served but
to serve others and to give his life as a ransom for many.”*

—Matthew 20:25-28

Day 1

There is only one effective method for building a healthy marriage. For many of us it's hidden in plain sight. We must warn you that this method isn't exciting, and it's definitely not easy. But it is the only way to apprehend the fulfillment, purpose, and love we all desire in our marriages. Are you ready for the great secret? Here it is: *serve*. The only way you can build your dream marriage is by dedicating your life to the service of your spouse.

Please resist the urge to put this book down or skip to the next chapter. We know the concept of serving doesn't typically evoke great excitement. It's more likely to inspire feelings of reluctance or even dread. We tend to recoil at the thought of being subject to another's interests, desires, or preferences. Yet Jesus, the Son of God and King of Kings, chose to become a servant in pursuit of what was best for us. Our best interests became His greatest concern. He rejected His rightful place of authority and privilege to bridge the chasm between God and man. And now that He has made a way of reconciling us to God, He delights in fulfilling our deepest dreams, desires, and joys by enabling us to live an extraordinary life and become like Him. Even as Jesus gave His own life away, He offered to make ours abundant. This unprecedented, limitless manner of service is the standard for how we should navigate all relationships, especially our marriages.

Now that the decks have been cleared, you have the opportunity to build the marriage of your dreams. But the only way you will realize your marital dream—that divinely inspired blueprint of bliss—is if you trade your life for it. In God's kingdom, you only keep the things you freely give away. The joy, love, and fulfillment you want in your marriage can only come when you sacrifice the pursuit of your best interests for the sake of your spouse's.

Have you noticed that the most miserable Christians tend to be the ones who are consumed with the pursuit of self? The most crippled of all are those who never do anything for anyone else. That's because in Christ, Jesus' spiritual DNA of serving is woven into our nature. Jesus is the ultimate servant. When we refuse to embrace our identity in Him—which includes, among other things, living as servants—we separate ourselves from His transforming power. This power is essential to constructing godly lives and marriages, and we can only access it when we seek to live as He lived. If we do not serve, we cannot build the marriages we want.

Becoming the Least

During His final meal with the disciples, Jesus told His closest friends that His death was imminent and He would soon be betrayed. How did they respond? First they ardently denied any chance of betraying Jesus. Then they quickly transitioned into an argument about which one of them was the greatest.

How absurd! Jesus was sharing details of His impending death, and all His closest friends could do was argue about their own greatness. Look how Jesus responded to their folly:

> "...Those who are the greatest among you should take the lowest rank, and the leader should be like a servant. Who is more important, the one who sits at the table or the one who serves? The one who sits at the table, of course. But not here! For I am among you as one who serves." (Luke 22:26-27)

Jesus' words probably hit the disciples like a soccer ball to the face. They'd made it clear they were interested in being great. Now He was telling them that being great meant they would have to excel at serving.

But Jesus didn't stop with mere difficult words. He proceeded to do something that made His disciples even more uncomfortable and confused. Scripture says:

> Jesus knew that the Father had given him authority over everything and that he had come from God and would return to God. So he got up from the table, took off his robe, wrapped a towel around his waist, and poured water into a basin. Then he began to wash the disciples' feet, drying them with the towel he had around him. (John 13:3-5)

What is astounding about this passage is *why* Jesus washed His disciples' feet. The answer is found by paying close attention to one word: *so*. Jesus had been given authority over everything, *so* He humbled

Himself and embraced the responsibility of a lowly servant. Jesus didn't struggle with false humility. He was obviously aware of His position of power. But instead of flaunting or abusing His far-reaching authority, He used His position as a platform for an unthinkable act of service.

In the first century, the roads weren't paved, and there were no malls where travelers could pick up a pair of Nikes. People wore sandals (or no shoes at all), so their feet were exposed to an abundance of dirt and animal feces. It's safe to say that in this environment, stinky, dirty feet were brought to a level unknown in the modern world.

Because of the abundance of dirty feet, servants or slaves were required to clean the feet of their masters and their guests. In a wealthy home, there were many responsibilities: stables to be managed, food to be prepared, rooms to be cleaned. But the job of foot washing was reserved for the lowliest servant. In some circles, the designation went even further, and this nasty task was exclusively assigned to the female servants, the only ones considered "unworthy" enough to do something so humiliating and disgusting.

Jesus chose to perform the basest act of service. Why? Because He needed His disciples to understand the importance of His lesson in serving. He even removed His robe, a symbol of His position as Teacher, and wrapped a towel around His waist in the fashion of a slave. Keep in mind that Jesus did all this to wash the feet of men who would soon deny, betray, or abandon Him.

After washing their feet, he put on his robe again and sat down and asked, "Do you understand what I was doing? You call me 'Teacher' and 'Lord,' and you are right, because that's what I am. And since I, your Lord and Teacher, have washed your feet, you ought to wash each other's feet. I have given you an example to follow. Do as I have done to you. I tell you the truth, slaves are not greater than their master. Nor is the messenger more important than the one who sends the message. Now that you know these things, God will bless you for doing them." (John 13:12-17)

After washing His disciples' feet, Jesus put His robe back on, resumed His role as Teacher, and put the finishing touches on a lesson His disciples would never forget. The eternal takeaways can be summed up in four points:

1. As Lord and Teacher, I am your ultimate example.
2. Since I willingly performed this lowly act, do not imagine it or any other act of service is beneath you.
3. I am your Master, One who is greater than you yet willing to serve as the lowest servant.
4. I bless those who follow My example of servant leadership.

Called to Serve

Jesus said that we will be blessed if we follow His example. This means His blessing will rest on our marriages when we imitate Him in the way we serve our spouses.

We are not encouraging you to imitate Jesus by way of initiating a nightly foot washing ritual. The point is to introduce His pattern of service into our lives. In marriage, we imitate Christ's example best when we use our respective roles as platforms for service. Paul wrote:

Don't be selfish… Be humble, thinking of others as better than yourselves. You *must* have the same attitude that Christ Jesus had. (Philippians 2:3, 5, emphasis added)

What was Christ's attitude? He chose to see Himself as a servant who elevated the best interests of others above His own. He took it to the extreme by dying for those He loved. Most of us will never be called upon to make that ultimate sacrifice for our spouses, but we have been called to forsake our self-centeredness on their behalf.

So if serving is so great—if it invites God's blessing—why aren't more people doing it? The problem is our fallen human nature, which constantly fights against the ways of God's Spirit and encourages us to make our own interests our goal. Our flesh demands that we acknowledge its desires, insisting that its cravings be fulfilled. But no matter how much we feed it, the human nature will always want more.

The sinful nature constantly promotes selfishness and discontentment, whereas God's Spirit empowers selflessness and offers lasting fulfillment. Each moment, we choose whether we are going to be led by God's Spirit or by the insatiable desires of our flesh:

> The sinful nature wants to do evil, which is just the opposite of what the Spirit wants. And the Spirit gives us desires that are the opposite of what the sinful nature desires. These two forces are constantly fighting each other, so you are not free to carry out your good intentions. (Galatians 5:17)

Jesus freed us from our sinful natures so we could freely give our lives away. Salvation didn't free us to get more; it freed us to give more! "For you have been called," wrote Paul, "to live in freedom.... But don't use your freedom to satisfy your sinful nature. Instead, use your freedom to serve one another in love" (Galatians 5:13).

We have been given freedom so that we can sacrifice our lives. If we live merely for ourselves, we squander our freedom in Christ and subject ourselves to the very selfishness and sin Christ died to liberate us from.

But by learning to live in service of others, especially our spouses, we take part in the abundant life He has made available.

Day 2

Filled with the Spirit

When people refer to the so-called "marriage passage" in Ephesians 5, they typically start with verse 22—the one that tells wives to submit. But Paul's exhortation actually begins earlier in the chapter. To fully grasp how our marriages are to portray the relationship between Christ and the Church, let's look back at verse 18:

> ...Ever be filled and stimulated with the [Holy] Spirit. (Ephesians 5:18 AMP)

In the original Greek, the word translated here as *filled* describes the process of being saturated with the Spirit as an ongoing experience. Once isn't enough. When we are not continually filled with and stimulated by God's Spirit, we will look to our spouses to fill needs only God can fill. No matter how great your spouse is, he or she can never replace God. If you expect your spouse to infuse your life with purpose and meaning, blessings only God can offer, then you will find yourself disappointed, frustrated, and unable to demonstrate the love of God.

Our marriages will only reflect Christ to the degree His Spirit is welcome in our lives. Christ is the cornerstone of our salvation, but the Holy Spirit is the agent of transformation. By allowing our lives to be continually filled with the Spirit, we can experience the renewing of our minds and the transformation of our behavior. God says:

Strip yourselves of your former nature... And be constantly renewed in the spirit of your mind [having a fresh mental and spiritual attitude], And put on the new nature (the regenerate self) created in God's image, [Godlike] in true righteousness and holiness. (Ephesians 4:22-24 AMP)

Trying to love and serve like Christ apart from His Spirit is like trying to get water out of a hose that isn't connected to a faucet. A hose cannot produce water on its own; it is merely a conduit. Likewise, only when we embrace the empowerment of the Holy Spirit can we love and serve our spouses the way God desires.

Willpower and behavior modification have their place, but ultimately they cannot renew our minds or overcome the desires of our flesh. Only as we embrace the Person and power of God's Spirit can we experience His life-changing influence in and through our lives—an influence that displays itself in Christlike attitudes and actions toward our spouses. Any attempt to modify behavior without the involvement of God's Spirit will lead to frustration and delusion.

We have received countless messages from men and women whose marriages were destroyed by manipulation and domination. In many cases, these individuals were knowledgeable of Scripture but lacked the Spirit's love and grace. As a result, the very words that were meant to liberate and empower were used to confine, undermine, or shame. Such evils are present wherever selfishness lurks. Selfishness will flourish when we don't avail ourselves to the work of God's Spirit and thus reject service as our primary marital role.

For the rest of this chapter, we will explore what serving looks like within the context of marriage. Our goal is to offer a biblical framework for how we can navigate and build our marriages through serving. In this spirit, we urge you not to use this chapter as a license to condemn any of your spouse's present or past behavior. Instead, use it as a framework to move forward.

We understand that we are framing these concepts under the premise that both spouses wish to honor God's plan for their marriage roles. We know this is not always the case. Whatever your situation, remember, you cannot change your spouse. If you try to do so, you will only get in God's way. Open your heart to the work of His Spirit, and give Him room to do what only He can do in your spouse.

Identities and Roles

To understand the roles of serving we take in marriage, we need to look back once again to the Garden of Eden:

> …God created human beings in his own image. In the image of
> God he created them; male and female he created them. (Genesis
> 1:27)

Both men and women are image-bearers reflecting the nature of God. Male and female are different, but they are equally important in displaying the nature of God on the earth.

Husband and *wife* are roles. They're unique roles, and the Bible gives specific input about what they entail, but these roles are not our identities. Our identities have to do with our original design. We were created as carriers of God's likeness on the earth. The Fall distorted this purpose, but the sacrifice of Christ restored it. Our salvation in Christ is first and foremost a change of identity.

No role—husband, wife, professional, minister, parent, friend—can trump your identity. And because a change in role (e.g., single to married) does not equate to a change in identity, both men and women are as valuable in God's eyes after marriage as they were before it.

Sadly, many people (especially women) feel that their value is altered after they are married. Women fear that to honor their husbands, they must become secondary in importance or contribution. In this scenario, rather than rise to acts of love and service, the woman shrinks in servitude until she all but disappears.

While it might initially appear that the husband benefits from this arrangement, he doesn't. In truth, both spouses lose when selfishness is fostered as a lifestyle. A husband who does not view his wife as an equal partner in marriage is not only robbed of an intimate ally, but he also loses one of his greatest opportunities for growth. Men become more Christ-like when they serve their spouses as Jesus serves the Church. Remember, Jesus modeled His headship by serving those He leads and loves.

Love, respect, and honor are essentials for both spouses. Both spouses matter and both spouses serve. Approaching marriage in this manner helps restore to men and women the power of dominion, God's gift of strength and authority that was entrusted to us from the moment of our creation.

Dominion vs. Domination

Then God blessed them, and God said to them, "Be fruitful and multiply; fill the earth and subdue it; have dominion over the fish of the sea, over the birds of the air, and over every living thing that moves on the earth." ...Then God saw everything that He had made, and indeed *it was* very good.... (Genesis 1:28, 31 NKJV)

In the beginning men and women were not enemies. They were intimate allies and co-laborers—two distinct persons unified with one heart. They were entrusted with the mandate to fill and subdue the earth. God gave them their commission (be fruitful and multiply) and let them determine the details. He gave them dominion.

Dominion is associated with ruling power, authority, or control. It describes an area of influence and is associated with possession of power. As we've learned from the story of the Last Supper, all authority, whether entrusted to a man or a woman, is given to serve others for their benefit and growth.

The battle of the sexes began after the Fall. With the overarching breach between God and His creation, dominion mutated into domination and manipulation. These perversions of God-given strengths continually war against His design for a beautiful union. Marriage became an instrument of division instead of multiplication.

Marriage was never meant to be a power struggle. It was created to be a power union. Marriage merges two people with very different vantages and strengths and then uses those differences to create the opportunity for multiplication. This is all part of God's plan to reconcile what seemed to be beyond reconciliation. Jesus said:

"For the Son of man is come to seek and to save that which was lost." (Luke 19:10 KJV)

We often understand this verse to be describing only evangelistic outreach when it carries a charge for so much more. Jesus did not come merely to save *the lost*; He came to save *that which was lost*. In the Fall, we lost our communion with God. But we also lost the oneness of our relationships with each other. This includes our relationships brother to brother, sister to sister, parent to child, and husband to wife. And we lost the beauty of our relationship with the rest of creation.

Jesus' work of salvation is about more than survival until heaven. It's about abundance and recovery in the now. Because of the cross, there is potential for restoration in every relationship that has suffered loss. This means we can experience healing in our marriages now. Men and women can again live as one!

When we are one in heart and purpose, we multiply; for God says that where there is unity, He commands a blessing (see Psalm 133). The enemy of our souls does not want us to experience the blessing of God, nor does he want us to multiply. He therefore does everything in his power to destroy our unity. By contending against the deception of domination and embracing the true nature of dominion, we partner with God to see His will enacted on the earth.

Now we will transition into a more targeted discussion of the different roles in which men and women serve in marriage. Without understanding God's perspective on identity, value, and dominion, one could easily err in thinking that these divinely established roles favor one spouse above the other. Having studied God's first mandate for marriage, and having recognized the difference between identity and roles, we believe you will see how exciting, weighty, and validating the roles of both spouses are.[1]

Day 3

The Husband: Honor Your Wife

In the same way, you husbands must give honor to your wives. Treat your wife with understanding as you live together. She may be weaker than you are, but she is your equal partner in God's gift of new life. Treat her as you should so your prayers will not be hindered. (1 Peter 3:7)

Honor goes both ways. The Bible makes it clear that both spouses are to honor each other, and we'll talk about the role of wives later on. For now, let's focus on the man's role.

Husband, your wife is not beneath you. She is your coheir in Christ, and you are to honor her as such. When Peter says that she is weaker than you are, he is referring to her physical strength, not her potential for insight, discernment, or spiritual power. Your wife's physical "weakness" does not make her less valuable than you; it only means she may not bench-press as much as you do. Peter's comment is a statement of factual observation, not a declaration of worth. This is an important point because we withhold service from those we do not see as being worthy of honor. Before we can lay down our lives for our wives, we must recognize their extraordinary value.

We are speaking about this directly, not because we believe you desire to belittle or neglect your wife, but because we cannot afford to be unclear. Men and women are both created in the image of God, so the expression of our Father is dishonored on earth when men do not honor, value, and protect women.

In the beginning, God said it was not good for man to be alone (see Genesis 2:18). His answer to this first problem—man's isolation—was to create Eve. Women are God-answers, not secondary creations. As a man of God, you have been entrusted with the opportunity to love, support, invest in, and serve your wife as a bold declaration of God's heart to a world that has lost its way.

Peter also wrote that men are to treat their wives with understanding. We have to seek to understand those who are different from us. All men are different, all women are different, and men and women are very different. I (John) don't dishonor Lisa because she is different from me. Instead I celebrate her and seek to understand what makes her different.

My life would be extremely monotonous and boring if Lisa and I were exactly alike. Though our differences have sometimes caused us hardship, they present opportunities for both our areas of weakness to be exposed, challenged, and strengthened. I need Lisa to be different from me. I honor her, and benefit myself and our family, by pursuing greater knowledge of what makes her tick.

Finally, note that 1 Peter 3:7 says dishonoring our wives will hinder our prayers. The well-being of women is so important to God that He has made honor and understanding of our wives foundational factors to our prayer lives!

The Head of the Union

For a husband is the head of his wife as Christ is the head of the church.... (Ephesians 5:23)

This verse does not speak of an issue of superiority and inferiority. It expresses a picture of Christ and His Bride, for that is what marriage symbolizes. Because husbands are aligned with Christ in this organic analogy, they take the role of leading their unions. They have the awesome responsibility of leading by serving as Christ does, so that the unbelieving world can witness the nature of Jesus. (And when you consider how profoundly Jesus loves the Church, you can't for a second truly believe He intended to lessen or marginalize wives by aligning them with the role of His Bride.)

The husband has not been given authority as head of his union so he can simply trump anything his wife says. On the contrary, a smart husband won't want to disregard his wife's input; he will realize that she is essential to the decision-making process.

In the early years of our marriage, I (John) prayed for about an hour and a half a day. It seemed to me that Lisa, who was working full-time, only prayed during the short time she spent in the shower or driving in the car. When we disagreed about a decision, I made the mistake of assuming that because I spent more time praying than she did, I could use my authority as head of our union to defer to my own judgment. Yet about half the times I handled disagreements this way, I would make a decision only to discover later that Lisa had been right!

To be honest, I was frustrated. *Why is Lisa's insight so accurate,* I thought, *when I am spending so much more time in prayer?* So one day I prayed, "God, I pray for an hour and a half every morning. Lisa prays for maybe ten minutes in the shower. Yet she's right about more than half of our disagreements."

In response, the Lord said, "Draw a circle." I found a piece of paper and drew a circle on it.

"Put Xs all over the circle," God instructed. When the circle was filled with Xs, He said, "Now draw a line right down the middle."

"Do you notice," God said, "about half of the Xs are on one side of the line and about half of the Xs are on the other side? John, when you were single, you were complete in Me by yourself. You were a full circle. But when you married Lisa, you became one flesh with her. Now that circle represents you both. You're one half and she's the other."

"Do you know what the Xs are?" God continued. "They represent information that you need from Me so you can make wise decisions. The problem is that you're making all your decisions based on only half of the information. You need to learn how to draw out of your wife what I show her so that you, as the head of the home, can make decisions with all of the information I give."

That revelation revolutionized my perspective on what it means for me to be the head of our marriage. I no longer desire to take advantage of my role to circumvent Lisa's counsel. I delight in benefiting from what God speaks through her, and I rejoice in the process of working toward unity in our decisions.

The Lead Servant

Again, the role of the man is not one of domination. Dominating is very different from leading. Leadership includes the dignity of choice, while domination demands without options. For men, the key to becoming godly leaders in our homes is in understanding what it means to hold a position of authority. Recall Jesus' words: "the leader should be like a servant" (Luke 22:26). As the head of the union, the husband is to be the lead servant.

Man is not the boss, with the woman *doing for him*. He is the leader who *does with her*. Actually, if he is wise, he will tell her repeatedly that he can't do *without her*. I (Lisa) love it when my husband tells me he needs me. It makes me feel uniquely empowered to meet whatever he lacks. And if I don't know how to be that woman, I will do all I can to find out how. I flourish when he calls me essential.[2]

Husband, serving your wife does not mean that you simply give her everything she wants. Rather, it means you lay down your life and make your decisions based on what is best for her. We are leading our spouses the way Jesus leads us. There are many things Jesus does in our best interests that we do not enjoy. You will inevitably encounter situations in which the welfare of your spouse conflicts with her preferences. By following Jesus' model, we know in such situations to choose what is best, not what is most comfortable or convenient. But the prerequisite to determining what is best for your wife is to love and honor her as Christ loves and honors the Church.

After washing His disciples' feet, Jesus made it clear that He was still their Lord. He never abdicated His position of power. But He did fundamentally redefine the purpose of power. As He displayed, we are given power in order to serve each other. Men, we are to use our authority as heads of our marriages to create environments that best serve our spouses. Since we are the heads of our unions, it is our responsibility to become the base servants. By doing this we submit ourselves to our wives.

> …Submit to one another out of reverence for Christ. (Ephesians 5:21)

Do you remember Paul's command in Ephesians 5:18 to "ever be filled and stimulated with the [Holy] Spirit" (AMP)? He follows this directive with a description of what a person filled with the Spirit will do, things like singing spiritual songs or giving thanks. Then in verse 21, he says, "Submit to one another." This is generally understood to be the beginning of Paul's discussion of marriage. But in *The Meaning of Marriage*, Timothy and Kathy Keller point out:

> *In English, [verse 21] is usually rendered as a separate sentence, but that hides from readers an important point that Paul is making. In the Greek text, verse 21 is the last clause in the long previous sentence in which Paul describes several marks of a person who is "filled with the Spirit."*[3]

Therefore, the Kellers say:

The last mark of Spirit fullness is in this last clause: It is a loss of pride and self-will that leads a person to humbly serve others.[4]

In the context of marriage, this means a spouse who is living by the empowerment of the Spirit (the importance of which we highlighted earlier) will be known by their submission to their mate.

Many people exclusively equate submission with the role of the wife, but Paul explicitly instructs both spouses to submit to each other. The Greek word for *submit* in this verse is the same Greek word used when Paul later commands wives to submit to their husbands. This word conveys subjection or subordination. As far as the authority structure of the home is concerned, yes, wives are to submit to their husbands as the head. But men are required to embrace another form of submission toward their wives.

Paul writes that we should submit out of reverence for Christ. The word *reverence* here is the Greek word *phobos*, and it conveys the idea of awe-inspiring terror or fear. (You'll notice that *phobos* looks a lot like *phobia*.) The word *reverence* doesn't do the original manuscript justice; a better translation would be "submit to one another out of awe-inspiring fear of Christ."

One day when I (John) wasn't being nice to Lisa, God spoke to me and said, "Lisa's my daughter first. She's your wife second." That put the fear of the Lord in me!

Husband, God is always present. He is aware of the way you speak to and behave toward His daughter. He sees through your words and into your heart's motives. Are you honoring Him by the way you treat your bride? If you dishonor your bride, you dishonor her Father. Care for her with fear and trembling.

Paul goes on to explain that a husband submits to his wife by laying down his life for her. In other words, he submits to her by subjecting himself to her best interests.

> For husbands, this means love your wives, just as Christ loved the church. He gave up his life for her... (Ephesians 5:25)

Christ never used His position of power for personal gain. He used it to empower us. Likewise, we as husbands are called to use our position of authority for the benefit and empowerment of our wives. Christ laid down His life to glorify and sanctify His Bride. His deepest joy—His happy ending, we could say—is in her glorification. There is no room for selfishness when you walk in the footsteps of Jesus. Your role as a husband is to spend your life serving your wife, for the ultimate purpose of revealing Christ to her and to the world around you. When you lead your wife this way, it will be much easier for her to take joy in submitting to your God-appointed position of authority.

Day 4

The Wife: Support Your Husband

> Wives, understand and support your husbands in ways that show your support for Christ. The husband provides leadership to his wife the way Christ does to his church, not by domineering but by cherishing. So just as the church submits to Christ as he exercises such leadership, wives should likewise submit to their husbands. (Ephesians 5:22-24 The Message)

You'll recall that Paul prefaced his instructions to husbands and wives by telling them to "submit to one another out of reverence for Christ" (Ephesians 5:21). In the next verse, he elaborates: "For wives, this means submit to your husbands as to the Lord" (verse 22). Many have seen this command as a loss for women, but it's not.

Because marriage is not about domination, the wife shares in the exercise of dominion as an equal partner. This does not conflict with the husband's headship, for both husband and wife have unique areas of authority and influence within their marriage and in the world around them. Dominion says, "I will exercise my authority and influence on your behalf, and you will exercise your authority and influence on my behalf."

The wife's support of her husband is an act of service. Wife, you have been entrusted with the heart of your husband. Protecting his heart by speaking the truth with love and respect can be one of your greatest acts of service. Learn to serve him by helping him express his heart. Rather than jumping to conclusions, help him grow in vision and purpose by enhancing his life with communication.

Women are vulnerable in the area of physical strength, and men often find their hearts at risk. Women are the caretakers of men's hearts, just as surely as men should be the protectors and providers for any physical weakness in their wives. Is there any commission nobler than to be the guardian of a heart?[5]

As the husband initiates service and lays down his life for his wife, she responds by honoring him as the head of the union. This is her part in revealing the love of Christ to the world. Her honor, love, and respect for her husband show what it's like to be led by Jesus. God has not asked women to submit because they are secondary. He is inviting them to display what the Church should look like. In marriage we have a chance to show what life can be like when we are led by a good, faithful, loving, and generous Lord and Savior. How tragic if we allow the enemy to pervert this into a despised or regretted role. In giving this role to women, God has asked His daughters to demonstrate that He is trustworthy.

God knows He made women strong and capable. Throughout history, He has chosen women to lead, judge, prophesy, intercede, and even to bear and nurture His only Son. In calling women to respect the headship of their husbands, He is not communicating that they are weak or unworthy. Instead He is saying, "I know you are capable and strong because you are My daughter. But in the eternal imagery of marriage, I need someone to show the goodness that is found in submission to Me. Will you willingly enter into the role of support and submission as a way of showing others I am deserving of devotion?"

The Burden of Leadership

Unlike God, husbands are not perfect. They don't always make the correct decisions, and they don't always serve their wives as they should. This can be a great source of frustration even to women who want to honor and support their husbands. Over time, they may be tempted to take matters into their own hands. Yet resistance to the husband's position of leadership, which may seem like a source of liberty, can actually bring women much pain and heartache.

When our firstborn son was still an infant, I (Lisa) was working long hours with a demanding schedule that extended into my weekends. I faced both professional and personal challenges at work, and at the same time I was striving to be the perfect mother and wife. Meanwhile, John was in a time of transition. While I was stressing out about my job and missing my son, John was working part-time, praying, fasting, talking to his friends, and playing golf. I felt enormous pressure and blamed it all on him. I felt that I was holding things together, and my grip was slipping.

I wanted John to worry with me, but he would not. When I voiced a fearful concern to my husband, he told me, "Lisa, let go of this and surrender it to God."

Never! I thought. *If I'm not taking care of all of this, it won't get done.* Tension gripped me like a taskmaster as inescapable pressures weighed upon me.

One night while in the shower, I complained to God about my heavy load. I couldn't give up any of my burden to John, I argued. I had to remind him even to take out the garbage. How could I trust him with anything more important? I wrestled back and forth, justifying why I could not relinquish control.

"Lisa, do you think John is a good leader?" the Lord gently asked me.

"No, I do not!" I asserted. "I don't trust him!"

"Lisa, you don't have to trust John," He replied. "You only have to trust Me. You don't think John is doing a very good job as the head of this home. You feel that you can do better. The tension and unrest you're experiencing is the weight and pressure of being the head of a household. It's a yoke to you, but a mantle to John. Lay it down, Lisa."

Immediately I understood the source of my burden. The headship of our home, which I'd been trying to bear, was oppressive to me because it was not my position to fill. It would not be oppressive to my husband, for God had anointed him as head of the home.

I recognized how I had jockeyed and fought for the lead position in our home. I had torn down my husband instead of building him up and believing in him. He, in turn, had relinquished his position of authority to me, and I had made a mess of it.

Broken, I turned off the shower and grabbed a towel. Immediately I found John in our bedroom. I wept and apologized. "I'm so sorry. I have fought you on everything," I said. "I was afraid to trust you. I'll quit my job tomorrow if you want me to. I just want to be one again."

"I don't want you to quit your job," John replied. "I don't think that's the problem. But I do think you need to quit thinking you're the source."

He was right. I was not our source; God was. Losing sight of that truth had made me stressed and unsupportive. We talked further, and I promised John, "I will get behind you and support you. I believe in you."

At the time I was not certain what I was supporting or believing in. I only knew John needed this support more than I needed all the details of what and why. I recognized that everything was terribly out of order in our home. I wanted God to bring order to the chaos I had created. In turn John also apologized for not leading and for withdrawing from me. We struck a covenant to love, support, and draw from each other.

That night was the first time in years I slept and actually found rest. My yoke of bondage had been removed.

Whenever we carry what God never intended for us to bear, we take up a heavy yoke of bondage. On the other hand, anything God has anointed us to do rests on us like a mantle, a sign of position and power that carries with it protection and provision.

By taking on the headship of our home, I had been yoked, and John had been dismantled. It was a mess! When I submitted to God's established order for the household, my yoke was broken and John was cloaked in God's mantle of leadership. I was covered also, for the mantle spread to cover and protect me and all persons under John's care.[6]

Day 5

Customizing Your Roles

The Bible has a lot to say about the roles of men and women in marriage, but there is a lot it doesn't say. In the same way that God told Adam and Eve to multiply and fill the earth without detailing the specifics, God gives our marriages boundaries without boxing us in. He provided the framework and modeled how we are to serve, but He does not micromanage every part.

You could liken this to being given a huge plot of land to landscape, build on, and enjoy however you'd like. Some people will want a pool, others might want to put in a basketball court, and some will want to do both or neither. Similarly, marriage is your "house and field" to build out and enjoy. If the wife is better at landscaping, let her landscape. If the husband enjoys gardening, let him garden. Both will enjoy the benefits of the other's service. No one has the right to say only the men can land-scape and the women should tend the garden. Do what works for you, always keeping in mind the framework of serving. The details are up to you, your spouse, and the guidance of God's Spirit.

One of the main sources of contention around the issue of serving in marriage is that we expect our spouses to serve us the way we serve them, and that doesn't always happen. In our family, we used to laugh when John told us he was a servant. He is notorious for disappearing from the kitchen as soon as dinner is over, leaving me (Lisa), along with our sons, to clean up and do the dishes. It didn't seem to us like he was serving.

We didn't recognize that John was serving in a different capacity. While we were clearing the table, he was overseeing our finances, opening mail, and paying the bills. He was opting out of a task we could manage without him to take care of other things that needed to be done—tasks that he, of all our family members, happens to do best.

That example brings us to an important point: the division of responsibilities. One of the most helpful things you can do to create a culture of serving in your marriage is to determine what each of you is responsible for. Knowing your agreed-upon responsibilities will aid you in two ways. First, good stewardship of your role is an essential part of serving your spouse. Taking care of your responsibilities provides your spouse with time and peace of mind. Second, when you know what your spouse is responsible to do, you know in what areas you can look for opportunities to go above and beyond in serving them.

You may have noticed that none of the verses in Ephesians 5 reinforce any stereotypes about the interests or skills of men and women. You need not feel any pressure to limit the allocation of duties in your home to what is considered "traditional" or "normal." Some husbands love to cook. Some wives enjoy car maintenance. One of you may enjoy supervising the kids' homework while the other would rather shuttle them to soccer practice.

Whoever is best with finances can be in charge of the money. That person can serve both by providing their spouse with spending money and by helping ensure the family stays out of debt.

You can also serve your spouse by taking care of your body, attending to your appearance, and not being swayed by the opinions of your friends at the expense of your mate's interests. You can serve with words and gestures as well as with actions. There's a lot of room to move in marriage, and there's a lot of opportunity to serve.

Enjoying the Blessing

"Now that you know these things, God will bless you for doing them." (John 13:17)

While service blesses the person who receives it, the greatest blessing falls upon the one who serves.

Your marriage, with decks cleared and vision cast, is poised to become a beautiful picture of God's love on earth. Your best approach to building it well is to take every chance you get to serve. Build each other and watch God's blessings flow.

When we started building each other, God began to build us. He expanded the boundaries of our world and allowed us to share His love and grace with many people around us. As you build each other through service, God will open opportunities for you to minister to those in your sphere of influence. His brilliant plan is to make your marriage into such a masterpiece that it turns the heads of even the most cynical unbelievers.

Serving is about both action and attitude. Every time you have occasion to serve your spouse, you can choose one of three responses: to refuse and opt for selfishness, to serve with a begrudging sense of obligation, or to joyfully lay down your life because you delight in supporting your mate.

You must have the same attitude that Christ Jesus had. Though he was God...he gave up his divine privileges; he took the humble position of a slave.... (Philippians 2:5-7)

When you marry someone, you in essence sign up to serve them for the rest of your life. Your "I do" was actually another way of saying,

"I am devoting my life to your best interests. I choose to rejoice in laying down my life on your behalf. Your dreams, desires, and goals are now of utmost interest to me. I want to learn how to display the love of God with you."

If you approach marriage from the truly humble position of a servant, you will experience a divine union. It won't always be easy, but if you contend for God's best and choose to live selflessly, your home will overflow with love, joy, peace, happiness, and fulfillment—and you'll give the world a picture of the love of God.

THE SECRET TO SUCCESS

"...I am among you as the One who serves."

—Luke 22:27 NKJV

...Don't use your freedom to satisfy your sinful nature. Instead, use your freedom to serve one another in love.

—Galatians 5:13

"Love is the foundation for marriage: love for God and love for another person," explain authors and speakers **Dr. Henry Cloud** and **Dr. John Townsend**. "It expresses itself in seeking the best for the other person no matter whether they deserve it or not. It places the other person above one's own selfish needs and desires. It sacrifices, gives, and suffers. It weathers hurts and storms for the long-term preservation of the covenant."[7]

Seeking the best interests of your spouse, placing their needs and desires above your own, and sacrificial giving all embody one thing: *serving.* This is the secret to a successful marriage.

Stop and think: What are some of your spouse's *interests*? What brings them fulfillment? What do they enjoy in terms of recreation and hobbies? What causes them to relax, smile, and feel happy?

_____

_____

_____

In what practical ways can you encourage them in their interests and make those interests a priority?

_____

_____

_____

Ask yourself and the Holy Spirit, *What's keeping me from serving my spouse? Is there anything specific in me that is fueling or promoting selfishness? Is there something I am afraid will happen if I humble myself and serve?* Pray for the Holy Spirit to show you your heart.

_____

_____

_____

Jesus is the ultimate servant, and as God's child, you have received His DNA. That's right! You have His spiritual genes—one of which is to serve. Take a moment to meditate on these verses.

> No one born (begotten) of God [deliberately, knowingly, and habitually] practices sin, for God's nature abides in him [His principle of life, the divine sperm, remains permanently within him]; and he cannot practice sinning because he is born (begotten) of God.
>
> —1 John 3:9 AMP

> Your new life is not like your old life. Your old birth came from mortal sperm; your new birth comes from God's living Word. Just think: a life conceived by God himself!
>
> —1 Peter 1:23 The Message

> "Come to me.... Take my yoke upon you. Let me teach you, because I am humble and gentle at heart, and you will find rest for your souls. For my yoke is easy to bear, and the burden I give you is light."
>
> —Matthew 11:28-30

What is the Holy Spirit revealing to you? How do these verses encourage you and motivate you to pray?

_____

_____

_____

EXERCISING DOMINION

What is man that You are mindful of him...?
You have made him to have dominion over the works of Your hands;
You have put all things under his feet...

—Psalm 8:4, 6 NKJV

Selflessness and a heart to serve are part of our inheritance as believers in Christ. These amazing characteristics of our heavenly Father are cultivated and made real in our lives as we spend time in relationship with Him. That is, our lives and marriages reflect the servanthood of Jesus to the same degree that we allow His Holy Spirit to continually fill us.

Reflect on the time since you began your relationship with the Lord. In what specific ways has His Spirit transformed you for the better? How has He transformed your marriage?

_____

_____

_____

By the indwelling of His Spirit, God desires for you and your mate to exercise dominion over all He has entrusted to you. According to Webster's original 1828 dictionary, the word *dominion* means "the power of governing or controlling; power to direct, control, and use; supreme authority."[8]

Carefully reread the definition of dominion. Now stop and think: Individually and as a couple, who or what has been placed under your control or in your care to direct, control, or exercise authority over? How are you doing in these areas?

_____

_____

_____

_____

Has any area of your dominion been twisted into something that now dominates and controls you? If so, explain.

_____

_____

Pray and submit this area to the Holy Spirit. Ask Him to forgive you and give you His grace (power) and a plan to regain dominion in that area.

In what practical ways can you work with your mate as an *ally* instead of an enemy? How can you better exercise dominion over your kids, your resources, your areas of work and ministry, etc.?

_____

_____

_____

_____

When you and your mate are one in heart and purpose, you multiply. Where there is unity, God commands a blessing (see Psalm 133). In what area(s) has the enemy been working overtime to cause division and strife between you and your spouse? Humble yourself and surrender these issues to God. Welcome His Spirit, ask for unity with your mate, and expect the Lord's blessing.

_____

_____

_____

_____

HONOR EACH OTHER AS EQUALS

...Each wife is to honor her husband.

—Ephesians 5:33 The Message

The same goes for you husbands: Be good husbands to your wives.
Honor them, delight in them. ...In the new life of God's grace, you're equals.
Treat your wives, then, as equals so your prayers don't run aground.

—1 Peter 3:7 The Message

Men and women are equal in marriage. The wife is not secondary to her husband, nor is the husband secondary to his wife. The two spouses are coheirs and have equal shares in the grace of God. How can we best honor each other as equals? By learning and living out our God-given roles.

Pastor Jimmy Evans shares that:

> "A man's foremost marital need is the need for honor. Isn't it interesting that God commands a woman to submit to a man 'as to the Lord'? When a woman *honors* a man and *submits* to him with a joyful attitude, she meets his deepest marital need.
>
> Likewise, when a man *sacrificially gives himself* to nourish and cherish his wife, he meets her deepest marital need—the need for security. A woman needs a leader who will *protect* and *provide* for her. When a man does this with a joyful attitude, a woman's inner longings are satisfied."[9]

Men, your wife is God's daughter first and your wife second. Women, your husband is God's son first and your husband second. We honor our heavenly Father by honoring each other as equal bearers of God's image. Carefully read God's instructions for husbands and wives in this passage:

> Wives, understand and support your husbands in ways that show your support for Christ. The husband provides leadership to his wife the way Christ does to his church, not by domineering

but by cherishing. So just as the church submits to Christ as he exercises such leadership, wives should likewise submit to their husbands.

Husbands, go all out in your love for your wives, exactly as Christ did for the church—a love marked by giving, not getting. Christ's love makes the church whole. His words evoke her beauty. Everything he does and says is designed to bring the best out of her, dressing her in dazzling white silk, radiant with holiness. And that is how husbands ought to love their wives. They're really doing themselves a favor—since they're already "one" in marriage.

No one abuses his own body, does he? No, he feeds and pampers it. That's how Christ treats us, the church, since we are part of his body. And this is why a man leaves father and mother and cherishes his wife. No longer two, they become "one flesh."

—Ephesians 5:22-31 The Message

What is the Holy Spirit showing you about the role of the husband? The role of the wife?

_____

_____

_____

Are you honoring your spouse by living out your God-given role? In what areas do you have room to grow?

_____

_____

_____

_____

Pause and pray, "Holy Spirit, what's keeping me from honoring my mate? What am I missing out on because of dishonor? What potential in my spouse have I left untapped? Please help me see their extraordinary value." Get quiet and listen. What is the Holy Spirit revealing to you?

A PICTURE OF JESUS

As the Scriptures say, "A man leaves his father and mother and is joined to his wife, and the two are united into one." This is a great mystery, but it is an illustration of the way Christ and the church are one.

—Ephesians 5:31-32

God designed the roles of husbands and wives. These roles are not about inferiority or domination. They are ultimately illustrations of the relationship between Christ and the Church.

Now that you have read about the roles of both spouses, compare what you studied in this chapter to what you may have heard or thought before. Was anything in this chapter different from what you've heard or believed? What challenges you? Encourages you? What do you want to study further?

_____

_____

_____

_____

Think about the role of the husband: to lead his wife by serving her as Jesus serves. In marriage, he provides a picture of the leadership, service, and love of Jesus. Men, what excites you about your role? Is there anything about it that makes you feel uncertain?

_____

_____

_____

_____

You were never meant to fill this role by your own strength. Pause and pray, "Holy Spirit, you are the Spirit of Jesus Christ, and you live in me. Teach me how to love and serve like Jesus. Give me the grace to lead well, make sound decisions, and honor my wife as an equal partner in our union."

Women, what excites you about the role of the husband? How can you honor your husband's role to bring about oneness in your marriage?

_____

_____

_____

Next, consider the role of the wife: to willingly enter into the role of submission and support, representing the Church's support and submission to Christ. Women, what excites you about your role? Does anything about it bring you feelings of fear or inferiority? Why?

_____

_____

Your voice, gifts, and contribution are valid and valuable. Take a moment to pray, "God, thank You for asking me to model the goodness found in submission to You. I will not allow anything but Your Word to shape my understanding of my identity. Give me the grace to serve and support my husband as I likewise long to serve You."

Men, what excites you about the role of the wife? How can you honor your wife's role to bring about oneness in your marriage?

_____

_____

_____

Talk about your responses to these questions with your spouse. Discuss your vision for establishing oneness in your marriage, addressing any concerns or necessary adjustments. If either of you has feelings of fear or uncertainty, go to God's Word. What does it have to say?

Pray this together: "Father, we thank You that You have honored each of us with a beautiful, weighty, and noble role in our marriage. Help us to serve each other and to model oneness and love well, for Your glory. In Jesus' name, amen."

TEAMING UP

Live in harmony with one another; do not be haughty (snobbish, high-minded, exclusive), but readily adjust yourself to [people, things] and give yourselves to humble tasks. Never overestimate yourself or be wise in your own conceits.

—Romans 12:16 AMP

You have probably heard it said, "There is no *I* in *team.*" This is true not only in sports but also in marriage. You and your team-"mate" each play a significant, needed role, and neither of you is superior to the other. "Being different should not be a problem in marriage," contend **Dr. Henry Cloud** and **Dr. John Townsend**. "When your mate has an alternative viewpoint to yours in parenting or home furnishings, you have been enriched. Your world has been enlarged."[10]

So, who plays each position best in your marriage? There will always be some sharing of responsibilities, and these assignments may adapt over time. But overall, who's better positioned right now to complete each task?

Take a team inventory. Create a roster for your home. Write out the different positions that need to be filled and assign the best player to each role. Some tasks may be handed off to one spouse or the other entirely. Others may be best handled when shared, with responsibility varying from day to day or week to week.

Here are some examples:

Car cleaning & maintenance	Meal planning & preparation
Vacation planning	Washing dishes after dinner
Budgeting	Vacuuming
Bill payment	Dusting
Laundry	Lawn mowing
Supervising homework	Gardening/pruning
Taking kids to school, games, etc.	Grocery/supplies shopping

Did you enter your marriage with any pre-conceived ideas about which tasks either of you "should" be responsible for? If so, what were they? Evaluate your answers in comparison with your roster. Do you see any areas where adjustments are needed?

_____

_____

_____

Discard the stereotypes. Don't let others define these details of your marriage.

Look over your roster again and compare it to your spouse's. Discuss your answers together. Then write out an agreeable list of responsibilities.

_____

_____

_____

_____

Let's see how inventive we can be in encouraging love and helping out....

—Hebrews 10:24 The Message

In what ways can you use your attitudes, words, and actions to support your mate in their responsibilities?

_____

_____

_____

DISCUSSION QUESTIONS

If you are using this book as part of the Messenger Series on
The Story of Marriage, *please refer to video session 4.*

1 | Jesus gave us a great example when He took on the lowest position of service and washed the disciples' feet (see John 13:1-17). While the need for foot washing is virtually absent in our western world, the need to serve one another remains. What are some practical ways we can imitate Jesus and symbolically "wash our spouses' feet"?

2 | *Men*, why is it important for you as a husband to view your wife as an equal partner in marriage (see 1 Peter 3:7)? What will happen if you don't? *Women*, why is it important for you as a wife to not withhold honor from your husband? What will happen if you do?

How do these answers put the fear of the Lord in you to live out your God-ordained roles by His grace?

3 | The marriage relationship between one man and one woman is meant to reflect the image of Jesus' relationship with us, His Bride. Describe who the husband and wife symbolize in the marriage relationship. How do the husband's and wife's roles reveal the love of Jesus toward His Church and toward unbelievers? How are we empowered to carry out our assignments?

Leaders: For the second part of this question, focus on Ephesians 5:18, along with Acts 1:8; Zechariah 4:6; James 4:6: Philippians 4:13.

4 | God wants us to be united, not divided, by our differences. Think for a moment: What would life be like if you and your spouse were exactly the same, having identical weaknesses and strengths? Describe this scenario, and then share some new ways you can appreciate and celebrate your differences.

5 | Knowing your agreed-upon responsibilities in your home is very helpful and important. Is this something you've established in your marriage? How can this knowledge help you create an environment of service, and at the same time strengthen your spouse?

CHAPTER SUMMARY:

- The most effective method for building a healthy marriage is becoming a servant to your spouse—learning to sacrifice your best interests in pursuit of theirs.

- Our marriages will only reflect Christ to the degree His Spirit is welcome in our lives. By allowing our lives to be continually filled with His Spirit, we can experience the renewing of our minds and the transformation of our behavior.

- Men and women are image-bearers reflecting the nature of God on the earth. Both are equally valuable, and both are entrusted with authority to serve each other.

- Husbands, God has entrusted you to provide for, protect, and empower your wife. You are to love and honor her by sacrificially laying down your life, putting her interests first.

- Wives, God has entrusted you to serve as the caretaker and guardian of your husband's heart. You're to honor him by submitting to his leadership as you would submit to Christ.

- Knowing your agreed-upon responsibilities in your home reduces conflicts, helps produce peace, and serves to create a team mentality.

Intimacy

Sex is for fully committed relationships because it is a foretaste of the joy that comes from being in complete union with God through Christ. The most rapturous love between a man and woman on earth is only a hint of what this is like.

—Timothy and Kathy Keller, *The Meaning of Marriage*[1]

...Oh, lover and beloved, eat and drink! Yes, drink deeply of your love!

—Song of Solomon 5:1

Day 1

Scripture is not shy in describing God's plans for lovemaking. In fact, it is rather explicit and at times borderline erotic. If you don't believe us, just spend a few minutes reading Song of Solomon with your spouse and see what happens.

Unlike many of us, God isn't ashamed of sex. He delights in its beauty and celebrates its purpose. God wants to be intimately involved in our intimacy. Sex within the marital context is not just good and permissible—it's sublime and encouraged!

"Drink deeply of your love!" Song of Solomon says. In other words, sex is mysterious and profound; there is no reason to settle for a superficial experience. Taste and enjoy intimacy's unparalleled satisfaction.

Sex is like hitting a relational refresh button, so it is not surprising that Scripture often uses water as a metaphor for sexual pleasure and fulfillment. Water is essential to the continuation of life. It provides refreshment and vitality. A healthy sex life isn't the full substance of marriage, but its value cannot be overstated. God intends for lovemaking to be celebratory, a wonderful reminder of the profound covenant that intertwines two lives.

And did you know that sex is good for your health? In addition to increasing your relational intimacy, it boosts your immune system, helps you maintain a healthy weight, lowers your blood pressure, reduces pain, and lowers the risk of heart attack—to name just a few benefits.[2]

Some factions of the Church have stigmatized the desire for sexual intimacy as a depraved, carnal appetite. Because of this, even sex within marriage has received a bad rap. Some would have us believe it is an act of obligation the wife performs on behalf of her husband. But the truth is that sex is for the enjoyment of both spouses! Some have stigmatized sex as a necessary evil tolerated for the sake of procreation. This misguided notion, along with Satan's manifold perversions of the sacred act, has caused many to view it with great apprehension.

Reproduction is one purpose of sex, but from the beginning God designed it to also be a source of bliss. "Let your fountain be blessed," Scripture directs, "and rejoice in the wife of your youth, a lovely deer, a graceful doe. Let her breasts fill you at all times with delight; be intoxicated always in her love" (Proverbs 5:18-19 ESV). Other translations of this verse say: *be enraptured* (NKJV), *be captivated* (NLT), and *be thou ravished* (KJV).

Clearly God is no prude. He created the sexual organs and is not embarrassed by their functions. He made sex and hardwired its sensations. Our pleasure is His delight. He doesn't want to curtail our sexual desires. He wants to sanctify them.

Sanctified Sex

Sanctification is the journey of holiness, which we could also say is the journey to God's best for our lives. Think of it as the extraction of the human nature and the infusion of the divine. Developing an awesome sex life (which is part of God's best for us) starts with embracing God's call to holiness in the bedroom. In doing so we will discover sexual gratification that transcends the limits of human imagination.

But God can only sanctify, or make holy, what we offer Him. Sadly, many of us refuse to present our sexuality to Him because we are ashamed of past mistakes or held captive by past abuses. These experiences cause us to view our sexual natures as unholy, so we try to shield these shadowed realms from the Holy One. It's surprising how quickly many forget that the Creator of sex has the power to redeem it and make it holy.

Shame wants to keep the focus on us and away from God. It entraps us in an attempt to cause us to reject God's mercy and grace. Ultimately, what looks like shame initially can actually turn into a form of pride. We insult God's mercy, as though what He did was not enough to heal this intimate area of our lives. We continue to hold our pain close rather than release it to the light of love. Those who feel God neglected to protect them in their sexual past are often afraid to invite Him into their present. The fact is, God didn't fail you; what happened was the consequence of fallen humanity. Don't let the shame of sin or abuse keep you from enjoying the full extent of marital intimacy and sexual bliss. God longs to heal every broken place and make it whole.

Like so many Christian couples, when we were first married, we assumed our marital vows would wipe clean the sexual slates of our pasts and set us on the pathway to paradise. We believed that because we loved and were committed to one another, no shadow from the past could cross the threshold of our future. We imagined that regular access to sexual intimacy would banish the selfish patterns or tainted shame. We were sadly wrong, and we will discuss our unique stories here in order to share the choices and revelations that brought us freedom.

Neither heritage nor failure can disqualify God's children from establishing a new sexual legacy. But only God can sanctify our sexuality and redeem our mistakes past, present, and future. And only by His grace does the marriage bed become a shelter of fulfillment and love.

Whatever your past, God desires to radically and completely restore your sexuality. His grace is greater than anything you've ever done or endured. But you cannot access His grace unless you first make Him Lord of your sexuality. Acknowledge your brokenness and give it to God. He will transform your sexual nightmare into a beautiful dream.

Honoring the Marriage Bed

Let marriage be held in honor among all, and let the marriage bed be undefiled, for God will judge the sexually immoral and adulterous. (Hebrews 13:4 ESV)

If there's a problem in your marriage, it will show up in your bed first. Lack of passion in the marriage bed is usually a sign of other issues, not of poor sexual performance. Hidden problems manifest in places of vulnerability, and we are never more vulnerable than in moments of sexual intimacy.

The most important principle in sexual intimacy is honor. Many mistakenly believe the marriage bed cannot be dishonored or defiled, so anything goes. There is nothing further from the truth.

We honor our marriages when we are single or engaged by remaining pure and reserved for our future mates. We honor our marriage beds after the wedding day by never allowing others in (committing adultery) and by not allowing anything else to detract from the beauty of sexual intimacy (such as pornography, perversion, or impurity).[3] The marriage bed doesn't sanctify ungodly sexual indulgences; rather, ungodly behavior defiles the marriage bed and keeps us from enjoying true intimacy. We also honor our beds by seeing them as places in which to serve our spouses' best interests, as we discussed in the last chapter. Serving our spouses sexually means honoring their needs within God's definition of holiness.

At times, we serve our spouses by having sex even when we don't feel sexy. The older you get, the less feeling sexy matters. You stop approaching sex as merely something that affirms your physical attraction to your mate. It becomes more of an intimate attraction. God created sex as a way for husbands and wives to connect with each other; don't allow insecurity to keep you from enjoying this connection. (In this same spirit of service, you should not pressure your mate into any act with which he or she is uncomfortable for the sake of your own pleasure.)

Because we've made our marriage bed a place of honor, we have better sex in our fifties than we did in our twenties—even though we looked a lot better in our twenties than we do now. Great lovemaking is not about how you look or how you perform. It's about who you are together.

When we make love, we are celebrating our more than thirty years of married life. Our joys, pains, struggles, and victories add meaning and value to our intimacy. Our spiritual, emotional, and physiological intimacy all culminate in godly pleasure and satisfaction. The sexual culture we have established in our marriage is a testimony to God's redemptive power, for we are far from where we began.

Day 2

Lisa's Story

John and I brought different forms of sexual sin and brokenness into our marriage. While John fought his unique battles, I had to wage my own intimate war. I never imagined the seemingly carefree sexual choices I made as a nineteen-year-old college student would come back to confront my freedom as a newly married twenty-two-year-old.

When my parents initially talked to me about the subject of sex, they explained that it was reserved for marriage, but they didn't tell me why. The way I remember it, the major emphasis was placed on the fear of catching an STD or the shame of an unwed pregnancy.

My parents' marriage was on shaky ground, and there seemed to be a lot of inconsistency between what was said and how they chose to live. Case in point, my grandmother and father each had multiple sexual affairs. The concepts of purity or virtue never entered the conversation. From my observation, it seemed the trick was to do what you wanted as long as you behaved responsibly and didn't get caught.

I adopted this logic as my own in college and paired it with a sense of morality I had formed in the company of my peers: I would only sleep with people I loved, and I would take sexual responsibility. One aspect of this "responsibility" was using birth control. On occasion, I even brought some of my less responsible sorority sisters to my doctor so they, too, could get on the Pill.

Then I met John, and on our first date, he led me to the Lord. I was twenty-one years old. I got born again, Spirit-filled, and healed all on that same night. During the course of our conversation, I said something ridiculous. I made the comment, "I'm so glad I was moral."

I have to wonder why I would have ever said something so stupid. I have no idea, except that I didn't understand the difference between *moral* and *holy*. Remember, I thought sleeping with people you loved equaled being *moral*. Even though I had been born again, in those first few hours, my mind was far from renewed.

Later on, when we began to date seriously, I hoped John would forget what I had said. Imagine my terror when he told me, "I'm just so glad that both of us have kept ourselves."

I wanted to yell, "That was an ignorant, brand-new baby Christian talking!" That was when I discovered how painful the consequences of my private choices could be to others.

Then the day came when I knew John was going to ask me to share his life with him, and I knew I had to tell him the truth.

I felt like I didn't deserve John, believing I had compromised the precious opportunity to build my life with a man who loved God and cared about me. I went for a walk and cried out to God. I knew I was forgiven, but I was overwhelmed with regret for the consequences of my sexual choices.

I went to John's apartment to talk to him. But before I could confess my shameful secret, he said, "Do you mind if I read you a scripture? I felt impressed to share it with you."

I nodded, and John began to read: "Therefore, if anyone is in Christ, he is a new creation; old things have passed away; behold, all things have become new" (2 Corinthians 5:17 NKJV).

"I know this sounds weird," he continued, "but I felt like God said to tell you old things are gone. You are brand new, and you are like… a virgin."

I thought I was going to throw up. "I'm *not* a virgin," I said. "That's what I was going to tell you."

John took me by the shoulders, looked me in the eyes, and said, "If God says you are, who are we to argue?" In that moment, all my shame washed away.[4]

Restoring Broken Sexuality

Still, I had awakened my sexuality in the realm of lust and not in love. When I entered marriage and wanted to love, I didn't know how. In my mind, sex was bad. It was wrong. It was forbidden. Now that we were married, sex was suddenly good and celebrated and godly. I didn't know how to make the transition.

John and I would be alone together, and I would suddenly experience a terrifying flashback of an image in some horrible X-rated movie I had seen five years earlier in college. Or I would find myself shutting down sexually with shame from memories of past sexual encounters with a former boyfriend. It was terrible.

When I should have been able to give myself freely to my husband with total abandonment, I found myself tethered to the past. John deserved all of me, and I was no longer capable of sexual freedom because of my previous violations. I wrestled with impure thoughts, images, comparisons, and shame. I struggled against them, but it seemed to be to no avail. It was in this season of my life that I learned about the power of breaking soul ties and generational curses.

We addressed family curses earlier in this book. As I mentioned, there was a history of immorality and unfaithfulness in my line, which I had to renounce. But I also had to break soul ties from past encounters so that my fragmented sexuality could be restored. Let's look at a scripture that addresses this:

Do you not know that your bodies are members of Christ himself? Shall I then take the members of Christ and unite them with a prostitute? Never! Do you not know that he who unites himself with a prostitute is one with her in body? For it is said, "The two will become one flesh." (1 Corinthians 6:15–16 NIV)

I am not calling my ex-boyfriends prostitutes, but the principle here is the same. I had been one with them, and now I had a covenant with another. With each joining and separation, my soul had been fragmented until I was no longer whole but broken sexually. When you are broken sexually, it makes it incredibly difficult for you to give yourself completely to your spouse, because you are not complete anymore.

In order to walk in purity and enjoy the gift of intimacy, we must be whole, and only God can restore us to wholeness where there has been brokenness. Only God can restore honor to our sexuality when there's been violation and dishonor. Only God can take the impure and defiled and make it holy and pure again. Only God can give us beauty for the ashes we bring Him.

If your sexuality has been broken because of past immorality (whether promiscuity, pornography coupled with masturbation, or any other impurity), we'd like to invite you once again to set aside time for a prayer of restoration. Again, please prepare yourself spiritually before you pray, and pray only with your spouse, close friend, prayer partner, or just the presence of God's Spirit. Speak aloud:

Heavenly Father,

Thank You for sending Your Son to bear the punishment for my sin. Because I am in Christ, all the old things have passed away from my life. All things are now new. According to 2 Corinthians 5:21, Jesus took on my sin so that I could become Your righteousness. That is what I am today.

Now I confess and renounce my sin and the sins of my forefathers for any and all involvement in sexual sin and all impurity, perversion, and promiscuity. (Be sensitive here to specifically name the sins you are renouncing. Speak them out before God without shame. There is nothing hidden—He knows each of them already and longs to remove their weight of guilt and shame from you. Then, when you are ready, proceed.)

Father, take the sword of Your Spirit and sever every ungodly sexual soul tie between me and... (listen to the Holy Spirit, and speak each name out as you hear it. It is quite possible the names may even be of those with whom you did not have intercourse, but with whom you were sexually or emotionally involved in a way that should be reserved for your spouse or Savior alone.)

After speaking each name out individually, pray this:

Father, release Your angels to retrieve the fragments of my soul from these people. Restore them to me by Your Spirit so that I might be whole, holy, and set apart for Your pleasure.

Father, I renounce the hold of every perverted and promiscuous image. Forgive me for allowing vile and perverted images before my eyes. I make a covenant according to Psalm 101:3, and I will guard the issues of my heart by way of the gateway of my eyes. I will not allow any vile thing before my eyes. I renounce every unclean spirit and command it and its influence to leave my life.

Father, wash me in the cleansing blood of Jesus, for it alone has the power to cleanse and atone. I consecrate myself now as Your temple; by the power of Your Holy Spirit, remove all defilement of the spirit, soul, and flesh from this sanctuary. Fill me to overflowing with the indwelling of Your Holy Spirit. Open my eyes to see, my ears to hear, and my heart to receive all that You have for me. I am Yours. Have Your way in my life.

Love, Your Child[5]

Day 3

John's Story

I technically kept myself for my wife, but I was bound to pornography coupled with masturbation. I brought these addictions into my marriage, thinking sex with my gorgeous wife would cure my impurity. It didn't. I continued to battle with lust for years after our wedding ceremony. My addiction greatly hindered our sex life. I was ashamed and confused. I did not want to be bound by lust, but no matter how hard I tried I couldn't get free. Something had to change.

In 1984 I was responsible for shuttling the guest speakers who came to our church. One day I opened up about my struggles to one of those guests, a godly man I deeply respected. He was known for his deliverance ministry. If anyone could help me, I thought, he could. I told him about my struggles.

His response was not what I expected. "Stop it!" he said. "You just need to stop it!"

"Okay," I said, "But will you pray for me?"

He prayed, but nothing happened. I thought, *Maybe I need to find somebody who has a stronger gift to help people get free.* But I couldn't think of anyone who had a deliverance ministry more powerful than his. I felt stuck in my sin.

About nine months later, a friend of ours allowed me to stay at his condominium for four days. I retreated to the property in solitude for the sole purpose of confronting my addiction. "God, this is it," I finally said, "This has to end!" That day—May 6, 1985—I was miraculously, completely delivered.

After a few months of walking in freedom, I asked, "God, I don't get it. Why didn't I get free when I was prayed for? I humbled myself by opening up to that great man of God. Why did the deliverance take so long?"

Immediately God directed my attention to a change in my prayer life. For a long time, the essence of my prayers was, "God, use me. Please use me." I was the center of my prayer life. All my prayers revolved around my well-being and my calling. My desire to be free from lust was not fueled by love for God or even love for Lisa. It was fueled by fear that my problems with lust would keep me from one day stepping into my calling. My self-centeredness obstructed my intimacy with God, and that lack of intimacy kept me from experiencing His transforming power.

Then I had a change of heart, and the core of my prayers became, "God, I want to know You. Don't let there be anything between us." I went from being self-centered to being God-focused. When I got my eyes off myself and onto the Lord, I opened my life to His grace. He delivered me and brought wholeness to my sexuality. I had embraced what Scripture calls *godly sorrow.*

Godly Sorrow

For the kind of sorrow God wants us to experience leads us away from sin and results in salvation. There's no regret for that kind of sorrow. But worldly sorrow, which lacks repentance, results in spiritual death. (2 Corinthians 7:10)

For years, I experienced sorrow over my addiction. As I mentioned before, I didn't want to be bound by lust and was disgusted by my behavior. Many people experience sorrow over their sin. But there is a godly sorrow that leads to repentance and transformation, and there is a worldly sorrow that leads to condemnation without change.

Worldly sorrow is self-focused and fueled by pride. It's marked by despair and self-loathing because it only sees the solutions possible within human limitations. It is blind to the hope found in the knowledge of God's power and will therefore invariably lead to spiritual death.

Godly sorrow, on the other hand, is not self-loathing or self-centered. It is God-centered. Even though it comes with pain, it carries hope for the future; for its strength is in God's ability to sanctify, empower, and redeem. Godly sorrow may sting for a moment, but joy and life soon follow in its steps.

Worldly sorrow and condemnation had strengthened lust's grip on my life. I thought I was being pious when I prayed that God would still use me, but I was actually being prideful. My desire to be free was about my interests. It had little to do with how I was hurting God's heart.

Many people desire freedom solely because they don't want their sins to create storehouses of regret, inhibit future success, or result in judgment. This fearful, self-protecting disposition will never produce the power to change.

We cannot become like God if we do not know and share His heart. Intimacy with Him is always a precursor to transformation. We gain and maintain freedom from sin by abiding in relationship with Him. As we draw close to God in humility, He will reveal Himself and empower us to be holy:

...."God opposes the proud, but gives grace to the humble." Submit yourselves therefore to God. ...Draw near to God, and he will draw near to you [reveal Himself to you]. ...Let your laughter be turned to mourning and your joy to gloom [godly sorrow]. Humble yourselves before the Lord, and he will exalt you. (James 4:6-10 ESV)

God exalts us by delivering us from the cravings and entrapments of our sinful natures. It is for freedom that He has set us free. But we cannot discover liberty until we have come to know the Liberator. If you desire deliverance, pursue God's heart. This closeness will fuel a deep, godly sorrow whenever you are not walking in His ways, which will in turn draw you deeper in relationship with Him and empower you to walk in freedom.

Remember, you are a child of God, and condemnation has no place in your life. If you falter on your way to experiencing freedom, don't allow yourself to dwell on your own inability. Do not fear the consequences of your mistake. Instead, dwell on God's greatness and the redemptive power of His grace.

> So now there is no condemnation for those who belong to Christ Jesus. And because you belong to him, the power of the life-giving Spirit has freed you from the power of sin that leads to death. (Romans 8:1-2)

Pornography and Intimacy

While I (John) naively thought my addiction to pornography would disappear after I was married, just the opposite was true. Many couples have experienced what I discovered: using porn adversely affects married men and women, not just singles. Its effects in marriage are always harmful, opposing a couple's ability to enjoy true intimacy.

Shockingly, we have heard reports of Christian counselors instructing married couples to view porn together as a sexual stimulant. This is a grave error. Don't do it. You will find in time that you awakened a sleeping dragon that will consume your intimacy with the fire of lust.

And "[the lust of] the eyes of man is never satisfied" (Proverbs 27:20 AMP). Pornography is a serious threat to marriage before and after the wedding ceremony. And whether we are with our spouses or alone, we were never meant to look on the shame of others.

While porn offers temporal stimulation and satisfaction because it appeals to the desires of our flesh, it will corrode our ability to be intimate with our spouses and with God. Eventually, it leaves us dissatisfied with our mates and ourselves. Porn may stimulate the sexual experience, but it will not address the underlying issues in a relationship. What appears to be a quick fix only adds burdensome weight to an already shaky foundation. While it may seem like pornography ignites a spark of life, it actually lights a deadly fuse that will eventually set off an explosion of confusion, distrust, and insecurity.

God intended sexual pleasure to be something you receive exclusively by giving yourself to the one to whom you've committed your life. This fosters intimacy beyond the marriage bed and enhances the whole marriage relationship. Indulgence in pornography, by contrast, is the pursuit of pleasure within the confines of self. It doesn't require intimacy, only an urge and an object of attraction. Pornography's pleasure is only a transient shadow of the euphoria experienced through God-designed intimacy.

When a couple brings porn into their union, they defile their marriage bed by including others in their intimacy. This was never God's plan. The sexual experience should be a reminder of the covenant that joins two lives, and the marital covenant has no room for a third party. What is sacred between two people becomes polluted among many. God wants us to honor the marriage bed—and the covenant it represents—because He desires it to be a place of wondrous delight and lasting satisfaction.

Day 4

Guarding Our Hearts

Until very recently, pornographic sites were the most popular online destinations. (They have just been surpassed by social media sites.) More than one in ten websites are pornographic in nature. Over 40 million Americans regularly visit these sites, and every second 28,258 Internet users are viewing porn.[6] Never before has sexual appetite been so perversely developed and indulged.

With the prevalence of counterfeit sexual stimulation, much lovemaking has been replaced by lust. Cyber-sex is destroying intimacy and ruining marriages. Even young men now struggle with erectile dysfunction because their sex drives have been warped by addiction to Internet pornography. Real women no longer satisfy them; their frequent virtual experiences are too different from real, fleshly encounters.

This is not an exclusively male issue, and pornographic content proliferates beyond the web. About one in five women view pornography online on a weekly basis.[7] Both men and women also feed their addictions offline with things like magazines or erotic books, the latter being especially popular among women.

Pornography and all other forms of sexual sin offer diluted pleasure outside of God's original design. But illicit sexual behavior, even if only in the mind or before a screen, has much deeper consequences than the perversion of gratification. Jesus said, "Anyone who even looks at a woman with lust has already committed adultery with her in his heart" (Matthew 5:28).

This form of unfaithfulness inherent in viewing pornography is a threat to marriage, for any perversion of God's intent for sexuality assaults the condition of our hearts. "Guard your heart above all else," Proverbs says, "for it determines the course of your life" (4:23). Sexual sin pollutes our hearts and can consequently destroy our lives and marriages. In sad confirmation of this truth, it has been reported that in fifty-six percent of divorce cases, one party had "an obsessive interest in pornographic websites."[8]

All sin is ultimately an attack on our vitality. Because we are Christians, the enemy has lost the battle for our spirits—so he is waging war on our souls. He wants us mired in the consequences of sin because he doesn't want us to experience life in its fullness (see John 10:10).

Christ set us free from sin, but we fail to experience this freedom when we allow sin to control our lives. For this reason, Paul wrote:

Do not let sin control the way you live; do not give in to sinful desires. Do not let any part of your body become an instrument of evil to serve sin. Instead, give yourselves completely to God, for you were dead, but now you have new life. So *use your whole body* as an instrument to do what is right for the glory of God. (Romans 6:12-13, emphasis added)

The *whole body* includes our sexuality. We glorify God when we give ourselves completely to Him and allow His Spirit to guide our sexual choices. He will set us free from what binds us and robs us of the life He intended. He will lead us into sexual expressions that bring liberty, intimacy, and delight.

We're not saying it's easy to overcome the tyranny of habitual sexual sin. "Work hard," Paul wrote, "to show the results of your salvation, obeying God with deep reverence and fear" (Philippians 2:12). Crucifying the flesh is a painful process, even though sanctification is a work of God's grace. At times the journey to holiness—and wholeness—requires steadfast resistance to temptation and pride. But if we allow the Spirit to do His sanctifying work in us, we will enter into spiritual joy that far exceeds the pain of the struggle.

A Vision for Purity

For I am jealous for you with the jealousy of God himself.
I promised you as a pure bride to one husband—Christ. But
I fear that somehow your pure and undivided devotion to Christ
will be corrupted, just as Eve was deceived by the cunning ways
of the serpent. (2 Corinthians 11:2-3)

Purity in our marriages is about more than just us. It is about Christ's
vision for a pure bride.

Currently, lust runs rampant in the Church. Recent research shows
that fifty percent of Christian men and twenty percent of Christian
women are addicted to pornography.[9] To combat this issue, many men
and women have turned to methods of accountability and behavior
modification to curtail their sexual addictions. This is a valuable sign
of desire to change, and these methods certainly have their place, but
accountability and discipline alone are not strong enough to overcome
the sin nature. If someone wants to engage in sexual immorality, no
form of natural restraint is going to hold them back. Even if their out-
ward behavior is temporarily controlled, their inner life will be ruled by
lust and condemnation.

Our behavioral patterns will truly change when our minds are
renewed. "Don't copy the behavior and customs of this world," Paul
implored, "but let God transform you into a new person by changing the
way you think" (Romans 12:2). As children of God, we are free from the
power of sin (see Romans 6:19-23). To enjoy this freedom, however, we
must first allow God to sanctify our behavior by renewing our minds.

Our minds are renewed when we spend time in God's Word and
in His presence. There is no other way. God's Word implanted in our
hearts, and established by His Spirit, provides freedom from sin (see

Psalm 119:11 and James 1:21). Many Christians lament their sexual shame but fail to bring that shame into the presence of the One who leads us into liberty.

Many religious institutions have tried to employ fear tactics and control mechanisms to rectify immorality. These efforts haven't worked and have led to an abundance of hypocrisy and sin. Shame drives sin into the shadows, where it thrives.

Religious laws and manmade rules cannot deliver us from sin. In fact, laws and rules create a breeding ground for iniquity (see Romans 7 and 2 Corinthians 3:6). God doesn't want us to be passionate about rules; He wants us to be passionate about Him. We are perfected in the experience of our Father's love and made whole through relationship with Him. Scripture says:

> And you know that Jesus came to take away our sins, and there is no sin in him. Anyone who continues to live in him will not sin. But anyone who keeps on sinning does not *know him or understand* who he is. (1 John 3:5-6, emphasis added)

The Greek word *ginōskō*, translated here as *understand*, means "to know a person through direct personal experience, implying a continuity of relationship."[10] Freedom from the sinful nature is found in personal relationship with God, not in secondhand knowledge of Him.

The apostle John, by the inspiration of the Holy Spirit, declared that a Christian who engages in habitual sin is not experiencing an intimate, personal relationship with Christ. The solution, therefore, to the struggles and sins that threaten intimacy in marriage is to grow in intimacy with the Lord.

If sin is controlling your life, run to God. Only in the experiential knowledge of Christ's love and grace will you be free from sin. When you turn to God in humility, He will renew your mind and remove the veils obstructing the knowledge of your freedom in Christ.

> But whenever someone turns to the Lord, the veil is taken away. For the Lord is the Spirit, and wherever the Spirit of the Lord is, there is freedom. So all of us who have had that veil removed can see and reflect the glory of the Lord. And the Lord—who is the Spirit—makes us more and more like him as we are changed into his glorious image. (2 Corinthians 3:16-18)

God doesn't want you to struggle with sexual sin—or any sin for that matter. He wants you to walk in wholeness and holiness. When your love for God grows—a love that is a response to the discovery of His love for you—your life will be filled with renewed perspective and desire to honor Him. In submitting to His will and ways, you will discover the power to live like Jesus. As Paul prayed for the believers at Philippi, we pray for you:

> …that your love will overflow more and more, and that you will keep on growing in knowledge and understanding. For I want you to understand what really matters, so that you may live pure and blameless lives until the day of Christ's return. May you always be filled with the fruit of your salvation—the righteous character produced in your life by Jesus Christ—for this will bring much glory and praise to God. (Philippians 1:9-11)

When we approach sex with a passion to please Christ, we can learn to enjoy intimacy with our spouses in every season of life.

Day 5

Seasons of Sex

To every thing there is a season, and a time to every purpose under the heaven… (Ecclesiastes 3:1 KJV)

In so many areas of life, timing is not just important—it is everything. If everything in life is seasonal and time is tied to every purpose, then our sexual expression is no exception. Each and every year is a collection of four seasons, and we believe each marriage is as well. So let's examine sex in light of this concept.

Spring: The First Decade

For illustrative purposes, we will liken each season of sex to a decade of marriage. For the sake of this example, let's choose a couple that marries around the current average age of twenty-eight. Then let's designate the first ten years of marriage (ages 28-38) as the season of innocence and new beginnings we know as spring. To quote Alexander Pope, this is when "hope springs eternal." In spring, your life is pregnant with possibility.

This first decade is a season of expectancy and discovery when you enter life with a new sexual perspective. What was dormant in your time of passionate waiting is now awakened in the spring of your marriage. You are both still discovering who you are as individuals and what it looks like to do life together. Every aspect of your sexual life together is fresh and new.

If you are planning to raise a family, more than likely this will be the season in which you experience the joys and challenges of pregnancy.

Your sex life will look and feel different with children in your life. You are no longer just lovers; you are father and mother as well. You may have children interrupting your rest or even sleeping in your room.

This can be a season of exciting challenges. I (Lisa) loved being a young mother. I loved nursing my children, and I breastfed each of my four boys for one to two years. Which brings up this point: in my zeal for nurturing them, I discovered it was much easier to neglect John. Young mothers should never be forced to choose between their children and their mates, but be careful that the baby you hold in your arms doesn't displace your husband.

I felt so fulfilled between nursing and cuddling my adoring babies that I wasn't making enough room for my husband. I forgot that even though he loved our sons, he wasn't getting the same intimate connection with them that I was. He needed me, but the needs of the children born from our love were so much more obvious than his were. In contrast, some husbands cater to their daughters, and while lavishing compliments on them, they forget to include their wives.

Be nurturing of your children and at the same time nurture your intimacy with each other. Invest in one another. Put the children to bed early enough to have time together. Share the load so you can share more than sleep in your bed. Talk openly with your spouse about your needs and concerns. Sometimes just saying, "I miss our intimate time together. How can we make it happen?" will go a long way toward dismantling any frustration.

Be intentional in your first decade to discover one another's intimate needs. Do not allow any sexual patterns to develop that either of you may grow to resent later on. Talk to one another. In this first decade or season of marriage, it is important to think of your intimacy as a garden that you plant well in spring in order to enjoy its fruit in summer and autumn.

Summer: The Second Decade

Summertime is always the best of what might be.
—Charles Bowden

If spring embodies hope, summer is vision alive and breathing. Life is so full in this season. Career paths are pretty well chosen by now, and you probably know if you are going to be parents. Any children already arrived are growing into the best of who they might be; and as the children are growing, the parents are also realizing who they are.

You do not want to miss one golden moment of summer! You will have to make time for intimacy to happen amid the busy sunshine of school, extracurricular activities, and careers. If your spring decade was planted well, you will enjoy this decade's season even more than the last. If your garden was not well tended in your first decade, it is not too late to plant.

Summer is a season when everything can grow quickly, including weeds. Do the work of keeping your rows clear of the overgrowth that can come out of familiarity. Continue to water what is healthy in your intimacy and it will grow even faster because you already have a decade of trust composting your soil.

Summer means long days, laughter, picnics, and afternoon thunderstorms. We discovered in our decade of summer that sex was best attempted in the afternoon. We were always too tired at night, and during the day when the boys were outside or at school was better than leaving it to chance in the evening.

Autumn: The Third Decade

Next is the decade we are calling autumn. So far this is our favorite season of all. We love the combination of brisk sunny days and cool nights. We are far more relaxed with our relaxed bodies.

Autumn is a second spring when every leaf is a flower.
—Albert Camus

We love this! Rather than trying to recapture your youth, celebrate your autumn. We find that in this season, intimacy once again has more room in our lives. In our fifties, our days have taken on a different rhythm. We are no longer doing homework with children or attending school or sporting events. We have more time for each other.

We are even now writing out the things we want to do in this autumnal decade so winter doesn't take us by surprise. One of those things is to take care of our sexual health by caring for our bodies with a healthy diet and regular fresh air and exercise. We are intentionally taking more walks together. This was what we loved doing when we were first dating.

Too many couples disconnect in the autumn of life. When their children move out, spouses discover they are living with a stranger. In this decade we all have a choice. We can mourn the loss of what was or choose to be excited about what will be. We encourage you to see this season as a chance to remake your marriage. You can become like newlyweds once again, except this time you will be both older and wiser.

Winter: The Remaining Years

In the depth of winter, I finally learned that within me
there lay an invincible summer.
—Albert Camus

We're not going to lie, getting old looks hard and extremely unfair. John's parents have done it well. Even though they have weathered some health challenges, their commitment to walking, exercise, and regular meals with friends has kept them spry, and the two cuties still sleep together in a double bed—by choice. Aging is best done together, and sex is magnificently beautiful when expressed in seasonal timing.

The author of our seasons verse in Ecclesiastes went on to say, "He hath made every thing beautiful in his time" (Ecclesiastes 3:11 KJV). The right thing in the right season is beautiful. We want to age well together and dance to the rhythm of our season.

One last example for thought. Speedo bathing suits are great for the Olympics, but I (Lisa) look away when I see old men in them. What once served the purpose of propelling you through the water with speed is unnecessary in the season of the relaxed swim and the float. The point is to never stop swimming. You don't cease to love water just because you no longer look good in a bikini. Swimming and sex are both fun in every season; it is just that they look different with the passing of time.

I started out in the spring of our marriage sporting a bikini, then moved into our season of summer as a mom in a one-piece. In our current season of autumn, I am all about board shorts and tankini tops. Who knows, as this next season called winter approaches, I just might wear a skirted bathing suit. But I will not stop swimming.

We may not swim as often as we did in our season of spring, nor swim mindful of the presence of our children like we did in our season of summer. But we will swim in our autumn and winter of life. In so many ways, sex is our eternal summer.

Practical Suggestions

No matter what season of life you find yourself in, talk. If you are single, share your desires and longings with God. Talk to a friend who shares your pursuit of virtue and encourage one another. If you are married, talk to each other. Share your concerns.

The truth is, everyone can become a better lover—but only if they are taught. Men can be methodical. They think, *If this approach has worked the last ten times, why change a good thing?* Women, tell your husbands if you want them to change it up. Say things like, "I love it when you kiss my neck." Don't make your husband guess. Openly share your desires.

Hold each other throughout the day when you cannot have sex so that you are comfortable embracing when you can. Cuddle. Go for walks when you need to talk about sex so no one feels like they are making a mistake in the moment. Don't believe what the magazines say; you have the right to customize your sex life as much as any other part of your marriage.

If you need help, get help. Do not leave such a sacred area of your marriage to chance. We have included a list of suggested resources at the back of this book, and your church can help direct you further.

Because this is not our area of expertise, just an area of limited experience, our insights apply mostly to couples who both want intimacy rather than simple gratification. We understand there are times when one spouse is completely uninterested in the other. We know this type of intimate rejection is extremely painful. Don't turn to another person; turn to God. Pour out your heart to Him and believe He will heal your union. Demanding sex from one another never works.

We also know there are seasons of challenge when a spouse is sick, discouraged, or has a medical condition that hinders or prevents your intimacy. Talk to your doctor to see what can be done.

Our prayer for you is that you will discover lifelong passion and create your own sexual legacy, established on God's holy design and unfettered by the wounds or failures of the past. May you "be intoxicated always" in each other's love!

A CELEBRATION OF INTIMACY

...Enjoy the wife you married as a young man!
Lovely as an angel, beautiful as a rose—don't ever quit taking
delight in her body. Never take her love for granted!

—Proverbs 5:19-20 The Message

God created sex *before* the fall of man. Within marriage, it is very good. In fact, it is extraordinary! There is no stronger bond of love and intimacy between a man and woman.

What attitude about sex do you bring to your marriage? Do you see it with the pure, positive image God intended? Why or why not?

_____

_____

_____

_____

Regardless of what your past has taught you about sex, your heavenly Father wants you to know that He fully approves of and blesses your sexual intimacy with your spouse. Take a few moments to meditate on these instructions concerning sex from God's Word:

> Let your wife be a fountain of blessing for you. Rejoice in the wife of your youth. She is a loving deer, a graceful doe. Let her breasts satisfy you always. May you always be captivated by her love.
>
> —Proverbs 5:18-19 NLT

> Husbands and wives should satisfy each other's sexual needs.
>
> —1 Corinthians 7:3 GW

> Let marriage be held in honor (esteemed worthy, precious, of great price, and especially dear) in all things. And thus let the marriage bed be undefiled (kept undishonored)....
>
> —Hebrews 13:4 AMP

Be honest. How do you see sex fitting into the portrait of your marriage? Has it been something you've tolerated or something you've celebrated? How do these verses help you see sex in a more positive light?

_____

_____

_____

God gives us a detailed picture of healthy sexual intimacy in Song of Solomon. Explore the excitement of this relationship, especially as recorded in chapters 4 and 7, and ask the Lord to adjust your vision and expectations of sex to line up with His.

The most important principle regarding sexual intimacy is *honor*. Is any of your current behavior dishonoring your marriage bed?

_____

_____

_____

In the *Amplified* Bible, Hebrews 13:4 defines *honor* not just as keeping the marriage bed undefiled, but as deeming marriage worthy, precious, of great price, and especially dear. What practical steps can you take to not only protect but also celebrate intimacy in your marriage?

_____

_____

_____

HEALING FOR THE BROKENHEARTED

*[God] heals the brokenhearted and binds up their wounds
[curing their pains and their sorrows].*

—Psalm 147:3 AMP

Most of us have hurts and pains from wrong choices we've made in the past, including sinful sexual choices. But our heavenly Father, in His incredible wisdom and intense desire to be in relationship with us, made a way to heal and restore our lives through His Son, Jesus. Paul encapsulates the story of God's love in his letter to Titus:

> It wasn't so long ago that we ourselves were stupid and stubborn, dupes of sin, ordered every which way by our glands, going around with a chip on our shoulder, hated and hating back. But when God, our kind and loving Savior God, stepped in, he saved us from all that. It was all his doing; we had nothing to do with it. He gave us a good bath, and we came out of it new people, washed inside and out by the Holy Spirit. Our Savior Jesus poured out new life so generously. *God's gift has restored our relationship with him and given us back our lives.*
> —Titus 3:3-7 The Message, emphasis added

Are there experiences in your past, or your spouse's past, that make either of you feel as though you don't deserve one another—or don't deserve to enjoy sex? Take a few moments to be still, pray, and think about this. If the Holy Spirit brings anything to mind, write it down and surrender it to Him in prayer.

_____

_____

_____

Get with your mate and share your hearts on this issue with each other. Pray and invite the Holy Spirit to heal your hearts and restore what has been lost.

God can only sanctify what we offer Him. Be honest. Are you withholding any area of your sexuality from Him? Is there a part of your sex life that you have made *off limits*? If so, what is it? Pray and ask the Holy Spirit to show you why you are withholding it. Write what He reveals.

_____

_____

_____

> *...Anyone united with the Messiah gets a fresh start, is created new.*
> *The old life is gone; a new life burgeons! Look at it!*
>
> —2 Corinthians 5:17 The Message

Our hearts are healed and made *whole* again when we give the Lord our *whole* hearts. That's what you've done by praying and releasing your past to God. Now, carefully meditate on the following: Deuteronomy 6:5; Psalm 119:2; Proverbs 3:5-8; Jeremiah 29:11-14; Mark 12:29-30. What is the Holy Spirit speaking to you about your marriage and sexuality through these verses?

_____

_____

_____

FREEDOM IN INTIMATE FELLOWSHIP

...Everyone who lives in union with Christ does not continue to sin....

—1 John 3:6 GNT

Intimacy with Christ, discovered through communion with His Spirit, is the foundation to freedom from all sin. Intimacy is *close fellowship*. It is the *one thing* King David, the apostle Paul, and Mary sought after.[11] Intimate fellowship is what it means to be *in Christ*—a phrase used nearly 100 times in the New Testament. Jesus described intimacy as *abiding* in Him. How do we gain and maintain an intimate relationship with Christ? By regularly giving Him our time and attention.

> "The secret place must have top priority in our calendars and schedules because it is the place where the incubation of intimacy is facilitated. ...The greatest dimensions of kingdom power will be touched by those who are truly ignited and energized by their *personal love relationship* with the Lord Jesus."
>
> —Bob Sorge[12]

Without question, freedom from sin is found in intimate fellowship with Jesus. So how would you describe your relationship with Him? How often do you give Him your undivided time and attention? What motivates you to seek His presence? What directs most of your prayers—your desire for other things or your desire to know God?

_____

_____

_____

If intimacy with Jesus is not top priority, don't feel condemned. Just be honest with Him and ask for His grace. Pray, "Lord, I love You and want to know You, but right now, my relationship with You is not what I know You want it to be. I need Your help. Open my eyes to see the incomparable value of knowing You. Show me my heart. What is keeping me from putting You first? What can I do to help fan the flames of love for You? I ask for your insight and grace, in Jesus' name."

Be still and listen for what His Spirit shows you. Write it down and ask Him for the grace to do what He says.

The things that keep me from putting God first are:

_____

_____

_____

My part in cultivating an intimate relationship with Him is:

_____

_____

_____

GET AWAY WITH GOD

One of the best ways to intimately connect with Jesus, encounter His heart, and experience new levels of freedom is by going away for a focused time of prayer and communion with Him. You might go on a retreat with your church, or you might schedule a trip just for you and your spouse. A few days alone with God—disconnected from the distractions that demand your attention in the day-to-day—can forever transform your life and marriage.

Find a time when you can get away and be with God. Put it on your calendar and make it a priority. Bring no agenda and no distractions— just a Bible, journal, and pen. Be ready to receive abundantly from the goodness of His heart!

> **Discover the wonders of the secret place.** Read more in: 1 Chronicles 16:27; Psalm 16:11; 27:4-6; 31:19-20; 91:1-16; Isaiah 40:31; John 15:4-8; Hebrews 4:16

CULTIVATING THE RIGHT DESIRES

But I say, walk and live [habitually] in the [Holy] Spirit [responsive to and controlled and guided by the Spirit]; then you will certainly not gratify the cravings and desires of the flesh (of human nature without God).

—Galatians 5:16 AMP

The purity of your marriage is ultimately about the purity Christ desires in His Bride. Sexual desires aren't bad—they are God's creation, and He celebrates them! But when wrong actions or influences defile our unions, they war against intimacy and pervert what God has called *good*. The key to cultivating the right desires is to *starve your human nature* and *feed your spirit*.

"While it is beyond doubt that the Bible has a favorable and positive view of sex—witness the Song of Songs, for instance—biblical writers are also acutely aware of the snare of sexual sin and our propensity to spoil the gift God has given us. ...[This] is precisely why the institution of marriage is so crucial as we seek to navigate the sea of sexual desire. It is the only context in which sexuality becomes spiritually meaningful and helpful."

—Gary Thomas[13]

What you take in through your eyes and ears you ultimately take into your mind and heart. Your eyes and ears are the entryways to your soul and spirit. Everything you see and hear feeds either the human nature or the spirit.

Stop and think. In what ways are you feeding your *human nature*? Are you watching or listening to movies, TV shows, or music that fuels the fire of impure desires? Are you "feeding on" books, magazines, or websites that are polluting your mind and heart? What about friends and other influences—are any of them encouraging the wrong attitudes or actions?

_____

_____

_____

_____

_____

Ask the Holy Spirit to reveal any unhealthy influences. What or who is He prompting you to stay away from?

Transformation of behavior comes when we renew our minds with God's Word. Meditate on these scriptures.

> ...For the Word that God speaks is alive and active; it cuts more keenly than any two-edged sword: it strikes through to the place where soul and spirit meet, to the innermost intimacies of a man's being: it exposes the very thoughts and motives of a man's heart....
>
> —Hebrews 4:12 Phillips

> So get rid of all uncleanness and the rampant outgrowth of wickedness, and in a humble (gentle, modest) spirit receive _and_ welcome the Word which implanted _and_ rooted [in your hearts] contains the power to save your souls.
>
> —James 1:21 AMP

> Is not My word like fire [that consumes all that cannot endure the test]? says the Lord, and like a hammer that breaks in pieces the rock [of most stubborn resistance]?
>
> —Jeremiah 23:29 AMP

ALSO CONSIDER: Joshua 1:8; Psalm 1:1-3; 119:103; Jeremiah 15:16; Romans 12:1-2; Colossians 3:1-5; 1 Peter 2:2

In what specific ways are you feeding your _spirit_ the truth of God's Word about sex, intimacy, and holiness? How can you increase your consumption of truth? Pray and ask the Holy Spirit to show you practical, creative ways to feed your spirit and cultivate the right desires.

_____

_____

_____

If you ask it of Him, the Holy Spirit will show you how to cultivate a passion for holiness and deepen the intimacy of your union.

COMMUNICATION AND INTIMACY

...As we lovingly speak the truth, we will grow up completely in our relationship to Christ, who is the head.

—Ephesians 4:15 GW

The key to amazing sex in every season of marriage is **communication**. In so many marriages, intimacy is "destroyed for lack of knowledge" (Hosea 4:6 NKJV). If the expectations and preferences of both spouses are not communicated regularly, problems will develop. As you and your mate lovingly speak the truth to each other about your sexual desires, you will grow in to the largeness of marriage God intended. Authors and speakers **Bob and Audrey Meisner** explain:

> "Being best friends and being transparent with each other are tremendous benefits to your sexual enjoyment. ...Transparent conversation about your expectations of each other as well as your struggles and challenges brings warmth and acceptance into your sexual relationship. Make it a priority to understand your spouse, who is different from you in sex drive, energy level and expression. And be patient; it will take a lifetime for you to know each other in every intimate detail."[14]

Complete these sentences:

"I understand that our best time to make love in this season is

_____"

"My mate feels safe and is most able to participate when

_____"

"I think our greatest obstacle to regularly making love in our season of marriage is _____"

"The most important thing I want to share with my spouse about our sexual intimacy right now is _____"

What I *Enjoy* Most with My Mate Sexually:

_____

_____

_____

_____

What I *Dislike* Doing Sexually with My Mate:

_____

_____

_____

_____

Have you ever openly and honestly shared your likes and dislikes with your mate? Since they cannot read your mind, we encourage you to plan a special time and place where the two of you can share your answers with each other in a safe setting. Remember, speak the truth in love and pray for God's grace to understand and appreciate your spouse's needs and desires.

Husband, are you giving more time and attention to your work or your children than you give to your wife? What can you do to better serve her sexual needs? Humble yourself before your wife and ask her for her input, then pray about this together.

_____

_____

_____

Wife, has your family or work taken priority over nurturing your sexual intimacy with your husband? How can you better serve his sexual needs? Humble yourself before him and ask for his input, then pray about this together.

_____

_____

_____

DISCUSSION QUESTIONS

If you are using this book as part of the Messenger Series on
The Story of Marriage, please refer to video session 5.

1 | According to Genesis, God formed man from the dust of the earth and afterward formed woman and brought her to the man. Carefully read Genesis 2:21-25. What stands out to you from this account of man's initial reaction to seeing and being with his wife? How were things different after they disobeyed God (see Genesis 3:6-8)?

2 | Do you believe God's mercy, forgiveness, and grace are available and able to deal with any sin? If so, why do you think it is so difficult for many people to receive freedom regarding their sexual sins? If you were talking with a person who was struggling with this dilemma, how would you encourage them to release the sins of their past and receive God's forgiveness and grace?

3 | In your own words, what does it mean to *honor* your marriage bed? What does it look like in practical terms? How is the marriage bed *dishonored*?

4 | Scripture talks about two specific types of sorrow we experience: worldly sorrow and godly sorrow. Discuss the differences between these—what are the characteristics and end results of each?

WORLDLY SORROW   GODLY SORROW

_____   _____

_____   _____

_____   _____

_____   _____

5 | Intimacy with God is the precursor to experiencing freedom from all sin, including sexual sin. Stop and think. What would happen if we were able to experience lasting freedom and deliverance from sin in our *own* ability? How would it change our relationships with God and others?

Consider: Is there any value in our own, fleshly ability? Check out Romans 7:18; John 15:5; Philippians 3:3; and 1 Corinthians 10:12.

6 | In addition to our intimate fellowship with God, what are some practical steps we can take to guard our eyes and ears, as well as our minds and hearts, from the perversions and impure images, standards, and behaviors endorsed by society? Offer suggestions of what we can do in private as well as in public settings.

Consider these scriptures:
"I will refuse to look at anything vile and vulgar..." (Psalm 101:3 NLT)
"I made a covenant with my eyes not to look with lust at a young woman." (Job 31:1 NLT)

7 | One of the keys to remaining sexually pure is to remain *sexually satisfied* within the safety of your marriage. Carefully read the candid instruction God gives us through the pen of the apostle Paul in 1 Corinthians 7:2-5. What is the Holy Spirit revealing to you in each of these verses? How does this passage change your perspective on sex in general and specifically on serving your spouse?

Leaders: Have group members read the same scripture passage in *The Message* version.

CHAPTER SUMMARY:

- God wants you and your spouse to develop an awesome sex life, which starts with embracing His call to honor and purity in the bedroom.

- Don't let the shame of sin or abuse keep you from enjoying the full extent of marital intimacy and sexual bliss. God longs to heal every broken place and make it whole.

- Great lovemaking occurs when both spouses are passionate about pleasing each other. Sexual intimacy connects you with your mate physically, emotionally, mentally, and spiritually, culminating in godly pleasure and satisfaction.

- While self-centeredness obstructs our intimacy with God and keeps us from experiencing His transforming power, God-centeredness and intimacy with Him activate His power in our lives.

- Our minds are renewed and our hearts are purified when we spend time in God's Word and presence. God's Word implanted in our hearts, and established by His Spirit, provides freedom from sexual sin.

- Every season of marriage is different, which means you will experience distinct seasons in your sex life. Each season has its own joys and challenges. Talk about sex openly and regularly in each season, and invest in your intimacy with one another.

SIX

Begin Again

It is only possible to live happily ever after on a daily basis.

—Margaret Bonanno

Day 1

When our sons were young, I (Lisa) read them a folk story about a poor man who had a vivid dream of finding buried treasure at the base of an apple tree. The exact location of the tree was unclear, but the dream filled the man's heart with hope.

This man owned a vast and ancient orchard that had declined in fruitfulness, which led him into a state of poverty. Before the dream, he had thought about selling the orchard. But after the dream, he began to work with intent and vigor. He understood that finding the right tree might very well require countless hours of hard labor. Undaunted, he undertook the task of systematically digging around each of his trees. Each tree that did not reveal treasure only served to highlight the possibility of finding treasure in the remaining ones. But when he had dug the final trench around the last tree and still had not found the treasure he dreamed of, he collapsed in discouragement and exhaustion.

It was only when the next spring came that the man discovered his treasure. He walked around the orchard and breathed deeply, the air heavy with the scent of apple blossoms. All of his ancient trees were cloaked in showers of flowers. Each fragrant bud held the promise of autumn apples.

The poor man discovered his treasure by tending what was always in his care. When he dug around each tree, he unknowingly aerated the roots and turned the soil. This process brought the trees into a new season of fruitfulness. What once was all but barren had sprung back to life. That year and for many more to come, he and his family enjoyed a harvest that exceeded their wildest dreams!

When we began our journey through this book, we likened marriage to a tree. When the soil around a tree is compacted, its roots become bound, and they cannot spread out to receive the water and nutrients the tree needs to flourish. The first five chapters of this book were designed to help you do the work of reinvigorating the soil. By removing the debilitating and constrictive effects of offense, fear, and selfishness, you have aerated your roots. Because you dared to dream and chose to establish values, roles, and goals, you should see the promise of hope on your branches and treasure in your future.

Every marriage holds the promise of a harvest yet unrealized. We do our part by guarding our hearts and homes, and God does His part by commanding a blessing on our unions. The sapling with its tender branches, the mature tree with its weathered arms, and yes, even the tiny seed yet to sprout—all have the power of potential. Our God takes the barren and makes it abundant. The old He makes new, and the dead He quickens to life.

Making All Things New

Love doesn't erase the past, but it makes the future different.
—Gary Chapman[1]

Let's turn our attention one final time to the garden where this all began.

> God created human beings; he created them godlike, reflecting God's nature. He created them male and female. God blessed them: "Prosper! Reproduce! Fill Earth! Take charge! Be responsible for fish in the sea and birds in the air, for every living thing that moves on the face of Earth." (Genesis 1:27-28 The Message)

This has always been God's purpose for us. Our pasts, our fears, and the pressures and distortions of our environment come to poison or dilute the Creator's original intent. Perhaps you have felt too far removed from Eden's assignment to believe it is rightfully yours. Take heart. Every life and marriage can be reborn and a new genesis embraced.

> And he who was seated on the throne said, "Behold, I am making all things new."… (Revelation 21:5 ESV)

God doesn't simply renovate the past. He makes all things new. He took the trees of Eden—those markers of our downfall—and reinvented them. He stretched His Son across a tree of death so He could welcome us into His eternal city, home to the tree of life whose leaves are for the healing of the nations. Nothing that was lost was beyond His power to redeem. This includes our marriages. He renews all things so that we can begin again.

Your past is gone. It's cemented in the annals of time and beyond the reach of human efforts. But there is One who exists outside of time, and He is not bound by its limitations. He is "the high and lofty one" who "lives in eternity" (Isaiah 57:15). God will redeem the faults of your past as He writes the story of your future. In God's kingdom, yesterday's pain does not prevent tomorrow's potential. Each day His mercies are new and His promises await you. He loves—and longs—to make impossible things possible for you.

> [He] is able to do exceedingly abundantly above all that we ask or think, according to the power that works in us… (Ephesians 3:20 NKJV)

The fruitfulness, effectiveness, and fulfillment God can bring—to you individually and to your marriage—are beyond anything you can comprehend. Think about the dreams, goals, and desires you have scripted for your marriage in the past days or weeks. God doesn't want to merely meet that vision. He wants to abundantly exceed it. He wants to deepen your intimacy and extend your influence so that your union establishes His heavenly kingdom on the earth. He wants to work in and through you in radical and unprecedented ways. Maybe you didn't dare to dream as you read the previous chapters. Dare to do it now!

A foundational principle of life with God is that though He does not need our assistance to accomplish anything, He welcomes our partnership. He does not require our aid, but He wants our involvement. We get to participate in the achievement of impossible things. That is what we ask you to do as you begin again in your marriage: to aim for what even at this moment might seem impossible.

One story in particular gives us insight into how the impossible may be achieved. It comes at a rather unlikely moment in human history, a time when mankind rebelled against God's command to fill the earth.

Instead of spreading *out*, our ancestors clustered together and attempted to build *up*, aiming for a place in the heavenly sphere much as Adam and Eve had in Eden. You may already know how God intervened at the Tower of Babel.

> ...The LORD came down to see the city and the tower, which the children of man had built. And the LORD said, "Behold, *they are one people*, and *they have all one language*, and this is only the beginning of what they will do. And *nothing that they propose to do will now be impossible for them*. Come, let us go down and there confuse their language, so that they may not understand one another's speech." So the LORD dispersed them from there over the face of all the earth, and they left off building the city. (Genesis 11:5–8 ESV, emphasis added)

This endeavor was not God-authored, but had He not disrupted their work, it would have been achieved because of two factors: a *shared language* and a *united people*.[2] If these two elements would have empowered the seemingly impossible for the disobedient, how much more might they enable those who are one flesh in Christ?

Having unified language and purpose will be essential to you as you begin again, embracing the "exceedingly abundantly above" God has for your union. Let's examine both dynamics, starting with language.

Day 2

The Language of Heaven

"...What you say flows from what is in your heart." (Luke 6:45)

Throughout this book, we have repeatedly highlighted the importance of letting God work in your heart first. Change comes when we yield ourselves to His Spirit and submit ourselves to His Word. As we have stated, behavior modification is no substitute for inner transformation. But as you begin to be inwardly transformed, your outer world will be remade. The first evidence of the work God does in your heart will be found in the words of your mouth.

In every situation we face, we have a choice: will we speak the language of heaven or the language of earth? Earth articulates the apparent reality. Heaven speaks according to a higher Source of truth.

"My thoughts are nothing like your thoughts," says the LORD. "And my ways are far beyond anything you could imagine. For just as the heavens are higher than the earth, so my ways are higher than your ways and my thoughts higher than your thoughts.

"The rain and snow come down from the heavens and stay on the ground to water the earth. They cause the grain to grow, producing seed for the farmer and bread for the hungry. It is the same with my word. I send it out, and it always produces fruit. It will accomplish all I want it to, and it will prosper everywhere I send it." (Isaiah 55:8-11)

To speak God's language, we must know His Word. It will transform our vision, causing us to see the unseen and speak forth what may yet be. It will transform our utterances into the dialect of faith, which is about more than positivity or emotional optimism. It is about firm belief in what has been promised.

Here are some examples of how the languages of heaven and earth differ:

Our earth says, "Divorce." Heaven says, "Union."

Our earth says, "There's no hope." Heaven says, "All things are possible."

Our earth says, "Rejection." Heaven says, "Acceptance."

Our earth says, "You owe me!" Heaven says, "I freely give."

Our earth says, "Vengeance." Heaven says, "Forgiveness."

Our earth says, "I won't be your slave." Heaven says, "I will be your servant."

Our earth says, "I despise your weakness." Heaven says, "I see your potential, and my love covers your weakness."

Our earth says, "You don't meet my needs." Heaven says, "I want to meet yours."

These words may be inspiring on their own, but they are lasting and empowering when rooted in the deeper truth of God's Word. We encourage you to embrace the language of heaven by learning to partner scripture with every attitude and declaration you bring into your marriage. As God's people we know that "our present troubles are small and won't last very long. Yet they produce for us a glory that vastly outweighs them and will last forever! So we don't look at the troubles we can see now; rather, we fix our gaze on things that cannot be seen. For the things we see now will soon be gone" (2 Corinthians 4:17-18).

The tongue holds the power of life and death, and by faith we can call even those things that are not yet apparent as though they are (see Proverbs 18:21 and Romans 4:17). Let God's Word shape your world.

Speaking the Truth

> ...Speak the truth in love, growing in every way more and more
> like Christ.... (Ephesians 4:15)

Speaking heaven's language always means speaking the truth. But not every manner of speaking the truth is right. To speak God's language means we speak the truth *in love*.

Many couples err by adopting one of two extreme approaches. Some spouses use God's Word to attack or belittle their mates. They speak the truth, but they speak it out of frustration, anger, revenge, or offense. Others don't want to cause pain or create conflict, so they suppress the truth that needs to be spoken and operate in a superficial, counterfeit love. Over time this inevitably fosters deep feelings of disappointment and offense, which eventually lead to a blowup of some kind. Neither of these approaches achieves what God intends—that we become more and more like Christ.

As a husband or wife, you are aware of your spouse's weaknesses in a way no one else is. You could easily take advantage of your unique knowledge to hurt, shame, or condemn your mate. But we've embraced a higher calling, haven't we? We've committed to be our spouses' greatest servants, to seek their best interests. Our words of truth can help our mates grow more into the likeness of Christ—but we will never speak words of eternal value if we use our tongues as weapons that wound.

If we want our marriages to be healthy, we will have to address destructive or wrongful behavior, but there is a right time and a right place to do so. Have you ever noticed that pointing out your spouse's shortcomings in the middle of an argument never leads to positive change? Instead, it typically incites worse behavior and harmful interactions. When you feel something needs to be discussed, wait until you and your spouse have calmed down. If the matter is serious, it might be a good idea to plan a date so you can express yourself in a more intimate setting. This fosters an environment in which your spouse is more likely to hear you.

I (Lisa) distinctly remember God once telling me, "Lisa, if you want to be heard, say it the way you would want to hear it." To this, we could easily add, "Say it *when* you'd want to hear it." The middle of a conflict is usually not the right time to offer constructive criticism. It's best to share correction when your spouse is at ease and receptive. When you are exhausted, it is time to give it a rest. Forgive, hug one another, and determine to begin the discussion again in the morning.

It is imperative that we express sensitive truths bathed in love. No one likes to be told about their failures or faults, but those who are teachable benefit from being made aware of the areas in which they have opportunity to grow.

Before you offer advice, check your motives. Ask yourself, *Am I sharing this from a place of love, or am I seeking my own benefit or protection? Am I truly concerned for my mate's wellbeing, or am I seeking revenge for the way I've been hurt?* If you're offering behavior recommendations in the middle of an argument, chances are those suggestions are rooted in selfishness. You are, after all, responding to how your spouse is making *you* feel.

It's very difficult to speak the truth in love when you're emotionally compromised. If, however, you hold your tongue, one of two things will happen: either you will realize you were wrong and will be thankful you didn't say anything, or you will be able to calmly and accurately articulate something your spouse needs to hear.

We have learned that it is always best to overlook minor offenses by entrusting them to God. But we realize that some hurts are hard to forget. In the case of habitual, destructive behavior, it is actually unhealthy to hold your tongue. But the need to confront is not a license to wound. You can speak the truth in love by:

- Examining your motives in the light of God's Word.
- Resolving conflict by attacking the problem, not your spouse.
- Controlling your tongue by not speaking destructively.
- Being merciful.
- Being honest.
- Answering gently.
- Constantly offering hope.
- Speaking in the manner you'd want to be spoken to.
- Choosing the words, time, and place for confrontation wisely.[3]

Solomon said, "As iron sharpens iron, so a friend sharpens a friend" (Proverbs 27:17). There is room for godly friction and even disagreement in our relationships. If handled correctly, these moments of friction will forge godliness in our lives.

It's important to address issues that could compromise the unity of your marriage. Small hurts can become deep wounds if not properly treated, and many times our spouses are unaware of the pain they are causing us. Discussing concerns out of love for God and each other helps us grow in unity and become better spouses.

Day 3

Languages of Love

So far, we have discussed language in a more or less traditional sense, focusing on the words we speak and how we speak them. Now we want to adjust our focus slightly and discuss a different aspect of *shared language*. In chapter four, we shared that our marriages will be stronger if we realize that our spouses may not serve us in the same way we serve them. Similarly, people give and receive love in different ways. An excellent book to help you interpret the various dialects of love—one that has benefitted our relationship greatly—is *The Five Love Languages: How to Express Heartfelt Commitment to Your Mate* by Gary Chapman.

To help you understand why this is so important, we are going to use our marriage as an example. My (Lisa) major ways of showing love are through quality time and acts of service. This meant that early in our marriage, I was busy doing things (laundry, laying tile, cooking, cleaning, caring for the children, painting, and gardening) to show John my abundant love for him. I also attempted deep, meaningful conversations as ways of spending quality time with John while I did the things I felt spelled *love*.

I (John) was not on the same page as Lisa. I show love differently, through physical touch and words of affirmation. Lisa was making great meals, pulling up carpet, and laying tile, but I wasn't hearing, "I love you." And while I was earnestly speaking encouraging words and offering her physical affection, she wasn't hearing, "I love you," either. It was as if we were both speaking a foreign language.

For a marriage to be healthy, both people should feel happy and well-loved, and everyone deserves to be loved in a way they can hear it. In light of this, there is nothing wrong with letting each other know how you hear love communicated. We encourage you and your spouse to learn about how you show love by reading Dr. Chapman's book or by taking the free evaluation at 5lovelanguages.com. Talk about your results. What might speaking each other's languages look like in your unique relationship? This conversation is best done in a kind, non-accusing way. Say things like, "I feel loved when you…" and then elaborate.[4]

Intentional use of words or actions that are custom-tailored to your knowledge of your spouse's manner of showing affection will expand the vocabulary of love in your union. This will strengthen the foundation you establish by using heaven's language and speaking the truth in love. Taken together, these factors form a shared language within your union.

Next, we will look at how you can build the second aspect that enables the impossible: unity.

Under Mission

One of the things Jesus frequently underscored during His ministry was the importance of being in unity. Take, for example, a story recorded in the Gospel of John. On the night He was betrayed, Jesus prayed that we would live in oneness:

> I'm praying not only for [my disciples]
> But also for those who will believe in me
> Because of them and their witness about me.
> The goal is for all of them to become one heart and mind—
> Just as you, Father, are in me and I in you,
> So they might be one heart and mind with us.
> Then the world might believe that you, in fact, sent me.
> The same glory you gave me, I gave them,
> So they'll be as unified and together as we are—
> I in them and you in me.
> *Then they'll be mature in this oneness,*
> *And give the godless world evidence*
> *That you've sent me and loved them*
> *In the same way you've loved me.*
> (John 17:20-23 The Message, emphasis added)

Unity displays God's glory. It attests to the power of His Son's work of reconciliation. While many have sought to prove the gospel by reasoning or forceful argument, the first and best evidence of God's love for the world is the way His love is displayed among His people.

Unity not only speaks to those outside God's kingdom; it also benefits us. It is in the place of unity that God commands a blessing (see Psalm 133). In this way unity is a double threat to the kingdom of darkness: it brings favor to God's people and at the same time compels the lost to take note of God's love for them.

It's not surprising, then, that the enemy will do anything he can to create disunity in your marriage—and any selfishness or fear you harbor will only help his cause. Because staying unified requires us to fight both our enemy and our human nature, it is hard work. It requires the grace of God's Spirit and an awareness of clear purpose that transcends the difficulties of the moment. It is with this in mind that we look once again to Ephesians 5:21:

And further, submit to one another out of reverence for Christ.

In an earlier chapter, we discussed the roles both spouses play in submitting to each other as selfless servants. Now we want to expand your understanding of submission and how it helps us to be one.

Consider this: the prefix *sub* means "under," and *mission* is an assignment. Put them together, and we can draw a conclusion that *submission* means "under the same assignment or mission."[5] You have already spent significant time documenting your marital goals and strategizing the steps needed to achieve them. Let this call to submission, therefore, serve as a reminder that every goal you have for your marriage falls under the ultimate aim of displaying the love and glory of God. Both spouses are subject to the authority of this God-given mission, and that is what compels us to be one.

This perspective is what enables both spouses to be strong in their marriage. Submission does not require one spouse to be strong and the other to be weak. Because marriage upholds a mission so great, and so much bigger than any of us, it takes two strong people to build a strong union. Please understand that in using the word *strong*, we are not referring to personality or physicality. We are discussing contribution. As we have stated before, marriage is not about domination; it is about dominion. It's about taking territory, not being territorial.

There are areas of our marriage, family, and greater influence in which I (John) am more skilled than Lisa. She gladly defers to me in those areas. Likewise, there are areas in which Lisa is much more skilled than me. In those matters, I gladly defer to her insight and expertise. We are united under the same mission, and our mission demands the best both of us have to offer.

John has always excelled at navigating our finances. He has never had any difficulty believing God will meet our needs and bless our lives. Every house we have owned, he has found. When he took over paying the bills, it was as though a boulder rolled off my (Lisa) shoulders. I had been navigating them because of John's heavy travel and office schedule. Seeing my frustration with the task, he offered to take it over. What was burdensome to me was easy for him. He excelled with house, car, and other large purchases. He also connected well with our boys through competition, games, and similar activities.

I, on the other hand, have navigated our home. I have always wanted it to be a space where family meals happen around the table. I love to feed my family, and I wanted my boys to invite their friends over too. I also wanted our home to be a place where John could decompress when he returned from a trip.

Find out where you and your spouse are best equipped to take the lead. Learn to defer to each other in your respective areas of gifting.

Willingly yielding to each other's leadership in areas of strength will enable you to accomplish your shared mission.

Day 4

Priorities

> Two people are better off than one, for they can help each other succeed. (Ecclesiastes 4:9)

Missions and priorities are not the same thing, but they do go hand in hand. Agreeing upon and supporting the same priorities is essential to preserving unity.

Our priorities are dictated by our greatest goal: to know and reveal the love of God. Because this is a mission every believer shares, we can all uphold the same priorities, even though the strategies to do so will look different from couple to couple and from season to season. We propose that you see your priorities this way:

1. *God.* God is not really "first." He is above all else, and relationship with Him is essential to success and faithfulness in every other area of life. He should encompass and inhabit each of our priorities. But for the sake of clarity, we will designate Him as first on this list. So, in a manner of speaking, God is foremost.

    But our relationship with God and the work we do for Him are not the same thing. It's tempting, especially for ministers or others who serve in the church, to prioritize the work of ministry above our families. Please do not allow your family to fall prey to this distortion.

2. *Spouse.* Again, there is potential for subtle but costly distortion here. Your children are important, but they should not be cared for to the neglect of your spouse. Your children will someday mature and leave your care, but you are in covenant relationship with your spouse for a lifetime. Make sure you build your life together in such a way that when your children leave home, the two of you are still best friends.

3. *Children.* The exact details of each spouse's involvement and role in parenting their children will vary from season to season, especially dependent on the next priority—your callings. If one or both of you work outside the home, you will have responsibilities in additional areas of business or ministry. If fulfilling your calling currently means staying home with your children, our distinction between this priority and the next is not as applicable. But as C.S. Lewis said, "The homemaker has the ultimate career."

4. *Calling.* In truth, your calling includes everything on this list—and everything in your life. But again, we will limit the scope of this term for clarity's sake. What we refer to as "calling" is what God has called you and your spouse as individuals to do in the realm of government, business, health care, education, ministry, the arts, media, or elsewhere.

   In our marriage, this happens to be an area that we share, but many spouses do not work or minister in the same realm of society as their mate. If this is the case in your marriage, you can still take interest in each other's work and lend one another vital support. As Solomon said, when two work together, they can help each other succeed.

5. *Rest.* Sabbath was ordained by God, not men. When we rest, every other priority flourishes. God wants our lives to involve regular rest and recreation—which are not the same as inactivity. We rest by making time for the things that restore us spiritually, physically, and emotionally. The important thing in marriage is that we find ways to share rest, not just to rest alone. For us, this has meant finding common ground and interests to enjoy together, like spending time in nature talking about our dreams for our family and ministry. Learning to rest and recreate together is part of merging two lives into one.

6. *Community.* In far too many marriages, husbands and wives maintain completely separate social lives. While it's important to have guy or girl time and to build friendships with people other than your spouse, in a healthy marriage, the spouses' social lives will intersect. Our friends play significant roles in encouraging, supporting, and strengthening us. Because we are one flesh, we should have plenty of friends who know and love us both.

We cannot stress enough how crucial it is to have friends who intentionally bless your union. We both have friends who serve very different roles in our lives. I (John) have golf buddies who I only share recreation with. I also have friends I golf with to whom I can pour out my heart and soul. The men I share my challenges and weaknesses with love both Lisa and me.

Because my (Lisa) life is so full and I don't golf, I really only have friends of the heart who challenge me to grow deeper in every area of love. They are women who understand the unique challenges that present themselves in my life and marriage. Some are the best friends during challenges that arise in ministry, and others are the best to consult when it comes to conflicts in relationships. We value all of them more than gold.

There were some people who were our friends in the past but whom we eventually had to distance ourselves from. They favored one of us over the other and didn't promote unity in our marriage. If a friend is not for you both, do not associate with them. They will inevitably create division in your union.

Choosing to Love

Since God chose you to be the holy people he loves, you must clothe yourselves with tenderhearted mercy, kindness, humility, gentleness, and patience. Make allowance for each other's faults, and forgive anyone who offends you. Remember, the Lord forgave you, so you must forgive others. Above all, clothe yourselves with love, *which binds us all together in perfect harmony.* (Colossians 3:12-14, emphasis added)

Love is what binds us together in harmony. It is the foundation of unity, the true key to seeing impossible things.

In Ephesians 5:28, Paul says that "husbands ought to love their wives." The word *ought* stresses that this is a very strong obligation. The greater principle being communicated—one that applies to both husbands and wives—is that we are to love each other regardless of how we feel.

Our culture portrays love as a feeling, one that cannot be controlled but only responded to. If we feel love, we act like those who are in love.

It doesn't take long to discover that the feeling of love is not always present, but love is always a choice. God *chose* to love us. If we will choose to love, feelings will ultimately follow our actions. Acts of faith—like showing love when there are no evident feelings—can move mountains. God longs to bless our actions. Dietrich Bonhoeffer said:

> It is not your love that sustains the marriage, but the marriage that sustains your love.

The only way your marriage can sustain your love is if your emotional and spiritual fulfillment come from communion with God's Spirit. When we rely on the wrong source—that of our own strength—our love will fail when tested by an absence of feeling. But when we are grounded in the love of God, our actions of love can keep us in unity when our feelings falter.

Make no mistake. Marriage is not meant to be void of feeling. But as C.S. Lewis put it:

> The rule for all of us is perfectly simple. Do not waste time bothering whether you 'love' your neighbour; act as if you did. As soon as we do this we find one of the great secrets. When you are behaving as if you loved someone, you will presently come to love him.[6]

You can continue to show love to your spouse even when you do not experience the feelings of love. You can choose to serve, celebrate, and support. When your life aligns with love, your emotions will eventually affirm what your actions display.

Day 5

Bringing Out the Best

Christ's love makes the church whole. His words evoke her beauty. Everything he does and says is designed to bring the best out of her…. (Ephesians 5:26-27 The Message)

"A wise woman," Solomon wrote, "builds her home" (Proverbs 14:1). Because wise women build their homes, wise men will build their women! By building each other up, we display Christlikeness to our mates. Discovering God's best for our marriages means bringing out the best in each other.

Our love for our spouses is an act of partnership with heaven, an agreement with the affection of God. God does not define your spouse by his or her weaknesses, but by His grace and love. God speaks to your spouse's potential and invites you to do the same.

As we mentioned, when Lisa was a young girl, she lost her eye to cancer. Because of this, she had a profound fear of ever being in front of people. I (John) knew about Lisa's fear, but I also knew that God had gifted her with extraordinary wisdom.

When I was a youth pastor, I would sometimes tell Lisa I wanted her to speak to the girls in the youth group. "Absolutely not!" she would protest. "I'm not a package deal. The church hired you as the youth pastor, not me."

I would listen to her objections, knowing they were rooted in fear and not in a desire to rebel against God's gift on her life. She was so afraid to speak, yet whenever she did, people would find me after the service to tell me how deeply her message had impacted them. So when she protested, I would reply, "Just be ready for me to call for you tonight."

I (Lisa) thought John was trying to make me into something I was not. He knew the youth group girls needed a female voice in their lives, but I felt profoundly disqualified. I didn't realize that in addition to looking for an example for them, he was trying to create an environment for my gifts to flourish. He saw something in me that I couldn't see in myself. And even though I would, at times, stay up all night begging John not to make me speak, he never stopped positioning me so that God could bring out His best in me. I hated it at the time. But looking back, it is so evident that he was lovingly pushing me beyond my fears and limitations.

Just as John helped me, I lent my strength to him in different ways. In the early years, I was very active in editing his books and making sure they accurately communicated his heart. So much of what we have had the opportunity to do together in ministry came about because we loved each other into growth.

Perhaps you and your spouse haven't learned how to bring out the best in one another. You may have even fallen into the opposite behavior, using your positions of intimacy and influence to tear each other down. Today can be the day of new beginnings. You can establish a new standard.

It's never too late to begin again. If you want to learn to bring out the best in your mate, please find a quiet, private time and place to pray with your spouse. Speak the following to God:

Heavenly Father, we repent for mistreating the union You have established between us. Our marriage is Your masterpiece, and we have not stewarded it with the honor it deserves. We thank You for Your new mercies over our lives that enable us to begin again. Holy Spirit, we ask You to give us the grace we need to see each other through Your love. Give us greater insight into how we can celebrate and serve one another. Give us eyes to see the gifts and strengths that You want to amplify in each of us, and show us how we can champion Your work. We believe we are better together than we were on our own. We want to grow into the fullness of what You intend for our lives and union, for Your glory. In Jesus' name, amen.

Next, we have included declarations for you to make directly to your spouse. Look into their eyes and say these words:

Husband:

Forgive me for using my strengths to oppress and hold you down. Forgive me for not speaking to your virtue, your beauty, your wisdom, and your kindness. Forgive me for not creating an environment in which you can flourish. Forgive my selfishness in our conversations, our time together, and our bed. I believe God can heal, restore, and glorify our union. I believe you and I can do anything through Him who strengthens us. We will take dominion, multiply, and be very fruitful together in the name of Jesus.

Wife:

Forgive me for using my strengths to point out your weaknesses. Forgive me for dishonoring you and being selfish in our communication. From now on I am going to use my words to build your life. Forgive me for the times I was not a safe guardian of your heart. I believe in you, and I believe in us. I believe God can make all things new. I choose to love and forgive you. It is a new day filled with mercy and truth. Let's love and dream again.

Dear friends, we believe all the best is still before you. By God's grace, your legacy, your intimacy, and your influence can exceed all your hopes and expectations. In union with one another, and by the power and inspiration of God's Spirit, you will write a story that conveys Christ's love on the earth—and delights the One enthroned above.

The commission to begin again is such a vote of confidence. This is not a once in a lifetime opportunity; it is a perpetual opportunity as long as there is life. *Begin again* means we live in the now by letting go of our yesterdays while setting our hearts for what is ahead.

All the things we've presented here will be no more than good ideas unless we turn our unions over to the One who is ultimately able. Jude 1:24-25 positions us for a revelation of all that might be:

Now to him who is able to keep you from stumbling and to present you blameless before the presence of his glory with great joy, to the only God, our Savior, through Jesus Christ our Lord, be glory, majesty, dominion, and authority, before all time and now and forever. Amen. (ESV)

God is our keeper. He alone can move our marriages out of every realm of shadow. He entrusts us with the joy and glory of marriage so we can glorify Him. Our lives are living, breathing messages to others who are watching for us to love and grow well.

Each spring is a new beginning.

> For behold, the winter is past;
> the rain is over and gone.
> The flowers appear on the earth,
> the time of singing has come....
> (Song of Solomon 2:11-12 ESV)

EXPECT GREAT THINGS

[What, what would have become of me] had I not believed that I would see the Lord's goodness in the land of the living! Wait and hope for and expect the Lord; be brave and of good courage and let your heart be stout and enduring. Yes, wait for and hope for and expect the Lord.

—Psalm 27:13-14 AMP

Your heavenly Father loves you and your spouse intensely. He wants your marriage to succeed. In fact, He is "[expecting, looking, and longing] to be gracious to you" (Isaiah 30:18 AMP).

The question is, what expectations do you now have for your marriage? What God-inspired possibilities are you praying and believing for?

_____

_____

_____

Take time to meditate on what God's Word says about expectations.

...For you did awesome things *beyond our highest expectations*, and how the mountains quaked! For since the world began no one has seen or heard of such a God as ours, who works for those who wait for him!

—Isaiah 64:3-4 TLB

The teaching of your word gives light, so even the simple can understand. *I pant with expectation*, longing for your commands. Come and show me your mercy, as you do for all who love your name.

—Psalm 119:130-132

All praise to God, the Father of our Lord Jesus Christ. It is by his great mercy that we have been born again, because God raised Jesus Christ from the dead. Now *we live with great expectation*, and we have a priceless inheritance—an inheritance that is kept in heaven for you, pure and undefiled, beyond the reach of change and decay.

—1 Peter 1:3-4

...For the Lord is a God of justice. Blessed (happy, fortunate, to be envied) are all those who [earnestly] wait for Him, who *expect and look and long for Him* [for His victory, His favor, His love, His peace, His joy, and His matchless, unbroken companionship]!

—Isaiah 30:18 AMP
[Emphasis added to verses]

Earlier in this book, we discussed the dangers of unrealistic expectations. Based on what you've learned from these verses, what are some benefits of having the right kind of expectations?

_____

_____

_____

The greatest expectations are those formed by knowledge of God's promises, character, and plan.

Nothing is too hard or impossible for God. Read Genesis 18:13-14; Matthew 19:26; Mark 9:23-24; Luke 1:36-37; Ephesians 3:20. What is the Lord showing you about His immeasurable power and ability?

_____

_____

See, I am doing a new thing! Now it springs up; do you not perceive it?...

—Isaiah 43:19 NIV

We serve a God who makes all things new. Do you want something in your marriage to be renewed? Do you need new love, new dreams, new unity, or new intimacy? You can *expect* your Father to do a new thing when you ask it of Him. Write down what you want to be renewed, then pray and commit it to God.

_____

_____

SPEAK LIFE

Words satisfy the mind as much as fruit does the stomach;
good talk is as gratifying as a good harvest. Words kill, words give life;
they're either poison or fruit—you choose.

—Proverbs 18:20-21 The Message

The language of earth or the language of heaven—which do you find yourself speaking most? While the first produces death, the second brings life. In every situation you face, you have the choice to speak one or the other. As **Pastor Jimmy Evans** shares:

"Communication acts as the bridge that connects the lives of two persons, making free access to the other person's heart and mind possible. Communication is not just important, but essential, to a marriage. ...Words possess incredible power—power to wound or heal, to destroy or build up. We must discipline ourselves to use words that build up, strengthen, encourage and heal."[7]

As we have learned, there is a time for everything—a time to speak and a time to be silent. Stop and think: What is the *worst* time to address a problem with your mate? What is the *best* time? Why?

_____

_____

_____

Briefly describe the most challenging situation you and your spouse are facing right now. What negative "go-to" words and phrases often spill out of your mouth when you talk about this issue?

_____

_____

_____

Pause and pray: "Holy Spirit, I no longer want to speak negative words. I ask You to help me remove fear and anger from my vocabulary. Give me positive words of life—the language of heaven—to speak in faith over our marriage. In Jesus' name."

You can expand your vocabulary in heaven's language by growing in your knowledge of God's Word. Carefully read the following passages. Then write out one or more positive declarations inspired by these verses that you can regularly speak over your marriage. We've filled in the first as an example.

SCRIPTURES	WHAT HEAVEN'S LANGUAGE SAYS
Proverbs 5:18-19	"My mate and I will enjoy each other sexually and be satisfied all the days of our lives."
Ephesians 4:15, 29	
Ephesians 4:26-27	
Ephesians 5:21-33	
Philippians 2:3-5	
Psalm 133	
1 Corinthians 13:4-8	

SPEAKING YOUR SPOUSE'S LANGUAGE

Go after a life of love as if your life depended on it—because it does....

—1 Corinthians 14:1 The Message

Love has many languages. Your spouse speaks one most fluently, and it's likely that you're most articulate in another. **Dr. Gary Chapman**, author of *The Five Love Languages*, explains:

> "Your emotional love language and the language of your spouse may be as different as Chinese from English. No matter how hard you try to express love in English, if your spouse understands only Chinese, you will never understand how to love each other. ...We must be willing to learn our spouse's primary love language if we are to be effective communicators of love. My conclusion...is that there are basically five emotional love languages—five ways that people speak and understand emotional love."[8]

According to Dr. Chapman, the five love languages are words of affirmation, quality time, gifts, acts of service, and physical touch. Many people, ourselves included, find that they have both a primary and a secondary love language. As we mentioned, you can learn more about your love languages with the resources provided through Dr. Chapman's book or website.

You can see the roles your love languages play in the dynamics of your marriage by answering these questions: *What does my mate do that makes me feel most loved? What do they fail to do that hurts me most deeply? What have I most frequently requested of my spouse: words of encouragement or appreciation, time together, special gifts, physical affection, or help around the house? In what way do I regularly express love to my mate?* Record your thoughts and impressions.

_____

_____

_____

Next, answer those questions again about your mate. Where are the differences most notable?

_____

_____

_____

Were you aware of the differences between the ways you and your spouse communicate love? If so, how has this helped your marriage? If not, do you now see that this has caused problems or misunderstandings?

_____

_____

_____

Talk with your spouse about the ways you both show and receive love. Ask your mate, "What are three practical things I can do to express that I love you in your language?" Write their response here.

_____

_____

_____

Take some time today to talk with the Holy Spirit about
the best ways to show your mate your love. No one knows
your spouse better than He does!

PRIORITIZE YOUR LIFE

I appeal to you, dear brothers and sisters, by the authority of our Lord Jesus Christ, to live in harmony with each other. ...Be of one mind, united in thought and purpose.

—1 Corinthians 1:10

There is so much power in unity! Our oneness with each other is God's way of revealing His love to those who don't yet know Him. Nowhere else do we have the same level of opportunity for unity as we do in marriage. As you read chapter two of this book, you established your shared vision and goals for your marriage. Now, as we near the end of our journey through *The Story of Marriage*, we encourage you to think about the daily priorities that support your mission.

The "first" and greatest priority in your life is your relationship with God. Why is putting Him first so vital, and what does honoring Him in all things look like for you? How does a healthy relationship with God positively affect your marriage, family, work, and everything else in your life?

_____

_____

_____

Fulfilling your God-ordained mission and goals means prioritizing your spouse, children, calling, rest, and community—in that order. Pause and pray, "Lord, are my priorities out of line? If so, where? Who or what is getting too much attention? Who or what am I neglecting? What practical things can I do to gain and maintain proper order?" Record the insights and action steps He reveals to you.

_____

_____

_____

_____

You've committed to support and celebrate your spouse for the rest of your life. Children leave home, careers change, and friendships come and go, but your marriage is a covenant designed to encompass every season.

Based on the current state of your relationship, are you and your mate positioned to end life as best friends? Are you invested in supporting one another's callings and careers?

_____

_____

_____

What practices in your marriage communicate value and encourage oneness? Are any of your attitudes or actions undermining your unity?

_____

_____

_____

Read Ecclesiastes 4:9 and Colossians 3:12-14. Then pray these words:

God, You chose my spouse and me to be holy and beloved. By Your Spirit, give me the grace to show my spouse mercy, kindness, humility, gentleness, and patience. Help me to better my spouse's life with my words and deeds. I believe that we are better off together than we were apart because we can help each other succeed. Give us the wisdom to prioritize wisely, that we might know You better and serve one another well. In Jesus' name, amen.

BRINGING OUT THE BEST

...Make the most of every opportunity. Be gracious in your speech.
*The goal is to **bring out the best in others** in a conversation,*
not put them down, not cut them out.

—Colossians 4:5-6 The Message

As husband and wife, you and your mate are *one*. This means you share in everything. When your spouse succeeds, you succeed. When your spouse is fulfilled and productive, you can be more fulfilled and productive. By bringing out the best in your mate, you bring out the best in yourself. That's how Jesus treats us, His Bride. Scripture says, "Christ's love makes the church whole. His words evoke her beauty. Everything he does and says is designed **to bring the best out** of her..." (Ephesians 5:25-27 The Message).

So, what are your spouse's gifts, talents, and strengths? Think about what they are really good at and what they enjoy or receive fulfillment from. What have others consistently praised and thanked them for?

The gifts, talents, and strengths I see in my spouse are...

_____

_____

_____

_____

If these strengths are already benefiting others in the context of work or service, how can you support your spouse's passions and commitments so that they can continue to grow? If you see that your spouse has a talent that is not yet in use, can you think of (or create) an environment in which that gift would flourish?

_____

_____

_____

_____

238

And let us consider *and* give attentive, continuous care to watching over one another, *studying* how we may stir up (stimulate and incite) to love *and* helpful deeds *and* noble activities...
—Hebrews 10:24 AMP, emphasis added

So then, as occasion *and* opportunity open up to us, let us do good [morally] to all people [not only being useful or profitable to them, but also doing what is for their spiritual good and advantage]. *Be mindful to be a blessing*, especially to those of the household of faith [those who belong to God's family with you, the believers].
—Galatians 6:10 AMP, emphasis added

Carefully meditate on Hebrews 10:24; Galatians 6:10; and Colossians 4:5-6 (found at the beginning of today's entry). In what practical ways might you stimulate and bring out the best in your spouse? That is, what can you *say* or *do* to encourage them to use their gifts and strengths? How can you bless them and see them grow?

_____

_____

_____

_____

Take time to share all of your answers today with your spouse. Ask for their response, and allow them to share their heart. On what points do you agree? What new things did you learn about your spouse or yourself? Pause and pray a blessing over your spouse.

"Study your partner. Study yourself. ...You may be surprised and amazed by what you discover. ...The adventure of marriage is discovering who your partner really is. The excitement is in finding out who your partner will become."

—H. Norman Wright[9]

DISCUSSION QUESTIONS

If you are using this book as part of the Messenger Series on
The Story of Marriage, *please refer to video session 6.*

1 | God's instruction to Adam and Eve was to multiply and fill the whole earth. After a few generations, there arose a society of people who did not obey this command. Carefully read Genesis 11:1-6. In what ways were the people *one*? If the oneness of disobedient people positioned them for success, what does this say about us, those who are one both in marriage and in Christ and who seek to obey God?

2 | Unity releases great power and rewards. Explore these passages and apply them specifically to your marriage relationship: Psalm 133; Matthew 18:19-20; John 17:21, 23; 2 Corinthians 13:11. What blessings can be birthed when you live in unity with your spouse?

3 | A person's last words are important, and in Jesus' case, they were also powerfully prophetic. Read John 17:9-11, 20-23. These words are what He prayed for us just before going to the cross. Notice the *oneness* He and the Father shared. What is the Holy Spirit revealing to you through this passage? How does it motivate you to pursue being one with your mate?

4 | God is the God of new beginnings! He declares that He is making all things new (see Revelation 21:5). He wants us to experience and share renewed fellowship, hope, faith, sexual intimacy, and dreams with our mates throughout our married years. In what practical ways can we as husbands and wives help promote newness in our relationships?

5 | Proverbs 14:1 says that a wise woman builds her home. This means a wise man will build his woman! Women, in what practical ways can you as wives build your homes? Men, in what practical ways can you as husbands build your wives?

6 | While some married couples work together in business or ministry, many do not. This makes it all the more important that they stay connected and encourage one another in their individual callings and interests. What are some practical ways husbands and wives can support each other and stay connected?

CHAPTER SUMMARY:

- In Christ, every marriage can be made new! His Spirit continually offers opportunities for new beginnings in every area.

- In every situation, we have the choice to speak the language of earth or the language of heaven. By faith, we can agree with heaven by speaking according to the promises of God's Word.

- The goal of marriage is unity. We must work toward oneness in all areas of life.

- As we pursue oneness with our spouses—by speaking the same language and pursuing the same mission— God's blessings come upon us and the impossible becomes possible.

- Genuine love between husbands and wives displays God's glory and love to the world. Our unity draws others to Jesus.

- A wise woman builds her home, and a wise man builds his woman. As each spouse speaks life to the other's strengths, they enlarge their lives and bring about God's will on earth.

APPENDIX

How to Receive Salvation

If you confess with your mouth that Jesus is Lord and believe in your heart that God raised him from the dead, you will be saved. For it is by believing in your heart that you are made right with God, and it is by confessing with your mouth that you are saved.

—Romans 10:9-10

*I*n order to share the love of God with your spouse, you must first receive His love and salvation through His Son, Jesus Christ. Through the death and resurrection of Jesus, God has made the way for you to enter His kingdom as a beloved son or daughter. The sacrifice of Jesus on the cross made eternal and abundant life freely available to you. Salvation is God's gift to you; you cannot do anything to earn or deserve it.

To receive this precious gift, first acknowledge your sin of living independently of your Creator (for this is the root of all the sins you have committed). This repentance is a vital part of receiving salvation. Peter made this clear on the day that 5,000 were saved in the book of Acts: "Repent therefore and be converted, that your sins may be blotted out" (Acts 3:19 NKJV). Scripture declares that each of us is born a slave to sin. This slavery is rooted in the sin of Adam, who began the pattern of willful disobedience. Repentance is a choice to walk away from obedience to yourself and Satan, the father of lies, and to turn in obedience to your new Master, Jesus Christ—the One who gave His life for you.

You must give Jesus the lordship of your life. To make Jesus "Lord" means you give Him ownership of your life (spirit, soul, and body)—everything you are and have. His authority over your life becomes absolute. The moment you do this, God delivers you from darkness and transfers you to the light and glory of His kingdom. You simply go from death to life—you become His child!

If you want to receive salvation through Jesus, pray these words:

God in Heaven, I acknowledge that I am a sinner and have fallen short of Your righteous standard. I deserve to be judged for eternity for my sin. Thank You for not leaving me in this state, for I believe You sent Jesus Christ, Your only begotten Son, who was born of the virgin Mary, to die for me and carry my judgment on the cross. I believe He was raised again on the third day and is now seated at Your right hand as my Lord and Savior. So on this day, I repent of my independence from You and give my life entirely to the lordship of Jesus.

Jesus, I confess you as my Lord and Savior. Come into my life through Your Spirit and change me into a child of God. I renounce the things of darkness which I once held on to, and from this day forward I will no longer live for myself; but by Your grace, I will live for You who gave Yourself for me that I may live forever.

Thank You, Lord; my life is now completely in Your hands, and according to Your Word I shall never be ashamed.

Welcome to the family of God! We encourage you to share your exciting news with another believer. It's also important that you join a Bible-believing local church and connect with others who can encourage you in your new faith. Feel free to contact our ministry for help finding a church in your area (visit MessengerInternational.org). We pray that you will grow in the knowledge and love of God every day!

Notes

Chapter 1
1. "Women of Working Age," United States Department of Labor, accessed March 14, 2014, http://www.dol.gov/wb/stats/recentfacts.htm#age.
2. Some content in this section was adapted from: Lisa Bevere, *Fight Like a Girl: The Power of Being a Woman* (New York: Warner Faith, 2006), 5-6.
3. "Ambassador," Dictionary.com, accessed April 19, 2014, http://dictionary.reference.com/browse/ambassador?s=t.
4. C. Soanes and A. Stevenson, *Concise Oxford English Dictionary* (Oxford: Oxford University Press, 2004).
5. "Verse 6a makes it clear that this creation ordinance remains in effect even after the fall of the human race, the giving of the law, and the coming of the kingdom with Jesus. Verse 6b puts forward the text made famous by thousands of marriage ceremonies—humans should do nothing to sunder the divinely ordained union of holy matrimony. Without vv. 4–6a one could imagine v. 6b implying that some marriages are not ordained by God; in context this view is indefensible. On the contrary, precisely because God wants all marriages to be permanent, we dare not do anything to jeopardize them." Craig Blomberg, *The New American Commentary* Vol. 22: *Matthew* (Nashville: Broadman & Holman Publishers, 1992), 290.
6. Soanes and Stevenson, *Concise Oxford English Dictionary*.
7. Linda J. Waite, Don Browning, William J. Doherty, Maggie Gallagher, Ye Luo, and Scott M. Stanley, *Does Divorce Make People Happy?* (New York: Institute for American Values, 2002), 5.
8. Timothy and Kathy Keller, *The Meaning of Marriage: Facing the Complexities of Commitment with the Wisdom of God* (New York: Riverhead Books, 2011), 64.
9. Gary Thomas, *Sacred Marriage* (Grand Rapids, MI: Zondervan, 2000), 21.
10. Charles R. Swindoll, *Growing Strong in the Seasons of Life* (Portland, OR: Multnomah Press, 1983), 13.
11. "Marriage Quotes by Max Lucado," Fierce Marriage, accessed March 7, 2014, http://fiercemarriage.com/quote-author/max-lucado.
12. Rick Renner, *Sparkling Gems from the Greek* (Tulsa, OK: Teach All Nations, 2003), 55.

Chapter 2
1. W. Arndt, F.W. Danker, and W. Bauer, *A Greek-English Lexicon of the New Testament and Other Early Christian Literature* (Chicago: University of Chicago Press, 2000).
2. Ibid.
3. C.S. Lewis, *Mere Christianity* (San Francisco: HarperSanFrancisco, 2001), 204.
4. Ibid., 124.
5. Ibid., 109.
6. 1.6% of Everest climbers perish during the journey, while 40-50% of first marriages end in divorce. Sources: (1) "Death on Mount Everest," About.com, accessed April 19, 2014, http://climbing.about.com/od/mountainclimbing/a/Death-On-Mount-Everest.htm. (2) *The State of Our Unions: Marriage in America* (Charlottesville, VA: The National Marriage Project and the Institute for American Values, 2012), 1.
7. Bob and Audrey Meisner, *Best Friends, Best Lovers* (Huntsville, AL: Milestones International Publishers, 2006), 52.

8. F. B. Meyer, *Abraham, Or The Obedience of Faith* (Chattanooga, TN: AMG Publishers, 2001), 70-71.

9. Andrew Murray, *Humility* (Fort Washington, PA: CLC Publications, 2006), 13, 42.

10. Bill and Pam Farrel, *Men Are Like Waffles—Women Are Like Spaghetti* (Eugene, OR: Harvest House Publishers, 2001), 140, 142-143.

11. H. Norman Wright, *The Secrets of a Lasting Marriage* (Ventura, CA: Regal Books, 1995), 70.

Chapter 3

1. "Clear," Oxford Dictionaries, accessed April 19, 2014, http://www.oxforddictionaries.com/us/definition/american_english/clear.

2. Mike MacKenzie, *Seatalk, The Dictionary of English Nautical Language* (Nova Scotia: 2005), keyword "clear the deck." www.seatalk.info

3. Lisa Bevere, *Be Angry But Don't Blow It!* (Nashville: Thomas Nelson, 2000), 56.

4. G.L. Borchert, *The New American Commentary* Vol. 25B: *John 12–21* (Nashville: Broadman & Holman Publishers, 2002), 311.

5. Bevere, *Fight Like a Girl*, 60.

6. Lisa Bevere, *Out of Control and Loving It!* (Lake Mary, FL: Charisma House, 1996), 106-107.

7. This section was adapted from: Lisa Bevere, *Kissed the Girls and Made Them Cry: Why Women Lose When They Give In* (Nashville: Thomas Nelson, 2002), 123-124.

8. "How common is divorce and what are the reasons?", Utah Divorce Orientation, accessed January 21, 2014, http://www.divorce.usu.edu/files/uploads/Lesson3.pdf.

9. "Quotes on Forgiveness and Unforgiveness," Daily Christian Quote, accessed March 22, 2014, http://dailychristianquote.com/dcqforgive2.html.

10. Joyce Meyer, *Battlefield of the Mind* (New York: Faith Words, 2003), 192.

11. "Expectation," Oxford Dictionaries, accessed March 25, 2014, http://www.oxforddictionaries.com/us/definition/american_english/expectation.

12. Patrick M. Morley, *Two-Part Harmony* (Nashville: Thomas Nelson, 1994), 138.

13. Ibid., 139.

14. "Quotes on Forgiveness and Unforgiveness," accessed March 24, 2014.

Chapter 4

1. Lisa wrote about this subject in *Fight Like a Girl*. Some of her words from pages 121-122, 128 are adapted here.

2. Bevere, *Fight Like a Girl*, 124.

3. Keller, *Meaning*, 47.

4. Ibid.

5. Bevere, *Fight Like a Girl*, 109.

6. Lisa shared this story in *Out of Control and Loving It!* (pages 87-93). Some of her words are adapted here.

7. Dr. Henry Cloud and Dr. John Townsend, *Boundaries in Marriage* (Grand Rapids, MI: Zondervan, 1999), 122.

8. Adapted from Noah Webster's 1828 *American Dictionary of the English Language* (San Francisco: Foundation for American Christian Education).

9. Jimmy Evans, *Marriage on the Rock* (Dallas: Marriage Today, 2012), 87.

10. Cloud and Townsend, *Boundaries*, 163.

Chapter 5

1. Keller, *Meaning*, 260.
2. "10 Surprising Health Benefits of Sex," WebMD, accessed April 12, 2014, http://www.webmd.com/sex-relationships/guide/sex-and-health.
3. Bevere, *Kissed the Girls*, 121.
4. Ibid., 178-179.
5. Ibid., 121-125.
6. "The Stats on Internet Pornography," Daily Infographic, accessed January 24, 2014, http://dailyinfographic.com/the-stats-on-internet-pornography-infographic.
7. "How Many Women are Addicted to Porn? 10 Stats that May Shock You," Covenant Eyes, accessed March 27, 2014, http://www.covenanteyes.com/2013/08/30/women-addicted-to-porn-stats.
8. Covenant Eyes, *Pornography Statistics: 2013 Edition*, 11. http://www.covenanteyes.com/pornstats/
9. Ibid., 18.
10. J.P. Louw and E.A. Nida, *Greek-English Lexicon of the New Testament: Based on Semantic Domains* (New York: United Bible Societies, 1996).
11. See Psalm 27:4; Philippians 3:10-14; Luke 10:39-42.
12. Bob Sorge, *Secrets of the Secret Place* (Lee's Summit, MO: Oasis House, 2005), 180, 182.
13. Thomas, *Sacred Marriage*, 205.
14. Meisner, *Best Friends*, 127-128.

Chapter 6

1. Gary Chapman, *The Heart of the Five Love Languages* (Chicago: Northfield Publishing, 2007), 72.
2. Lisa Bevere, *Girls with Swords: How to Carry Your Cross Like a Hero* (Colorado Springs, CO: WaterBrook Press, 2013), 127.
3. Bevere, *Be Angry*, 120.
4. Some content in this section was adapted from: Lisa Bevere, *Nurture: Give and Get What You Need to Flourish* (New York: FaithWords, 2008), 166-168.
5. Lisa Bevere, *Lioness Arising: Wake Up and Change Your World* (Colorado Springs, CO: WaterBrook Press, 2010), 94.
6. Lewis, *Mere*, 131.
7. Evans, *Marriage on the Rock*, 213.
8. Gary Chapman, *The Five Love Languages* (Chicago: Northfield Publishing, 1995), 15.
9. Wright, *Secrets*, 129.

SUGGESTED RESOURCES

Select resources to help restore sexual brokenness,
protect intimacy, and heal hurting hearts.

BOOKS

Kissed the Girls and Made Them Cry: Why Women Lose When They Give In by
Lisa Bevere (Thomas Nelson, 2002)

Jailbreak: Breaking Free from the Prison of Porn by Vincent and Allison
Newfield (New Fields Creative Services, 2014)

The Purity Principle: God's Safeguards for Life's Dangerous Trails by Randy
Alcorn (Multnomah Books, 2003)

*Every Man's Battle: Winning the War on Sexual Temptation One Victory
at a Time* by Stephen Arterburn and Fred Stoeker with Mike Yorkey
(WaterBrook Press, 2000)

*Every Woman's Battle: Discovering God's Plan for Sexual and Emotional
Fulfillment* by Shannon Ethridge (WaterBrook Press, 2003)

Sexual Addiction: One Couple's Journey to Discover Strategies for Healing by
Gary and Sharon Worrell (Selah Publications, 2012)

Torn Asunder: Recovering from an Extramarital Affair by Pastor Dave Carder
(Moody Publishers, 2008)

Boundaries in Marriage by Dr. Henry Cloud and Dr. John Townsend
(Zondervan, 1999)

ORGANIZATIONS

New Life Ministries – NewLife.com
Resources for men and women, including national call-in radio and TV talk
shows, workshops, and counseling network

Heart to Heart Counseling Center – DrDougWeiss.com
Resources for men and women, including counseling, conferences and
intensives, and more

INTERNET FILTERING

CovenantEyes.com
Internet accountability and web filtering for individuals and families

WEEKEND EXPERIENCE

VISIT MSERIES.TV TO LEARN HOW TO USE *THE STORY OF MARRIAGE*
FOR YOUR CONFERENCE OR WEEKEND EVENT

 The M Series

The M Series is designed to support churches and individuals as they explore foundational concepts of Christian life. Each M Series message unpacks a biblical perspective on a single subject. These topical studies can be completed in six weeks or less.

THE STORY OF MARRIAGE

Marriage is God's masterpiece. He created it to express a much bigger story: His relentless, loving commitment to bring out the best in us. The dynamics of marriage have something to teach all of us. Whether married, single, or engaged, your story is ultimately part of the divine story of marriage.

Included inside:

- 6 sessions on 2 DVDs and 3 CDs (30 minutes each)
- *The Story of Marriage* interactive book
- Promotional materials

THE HOLY SPIRIT

AN INTRODUCTION

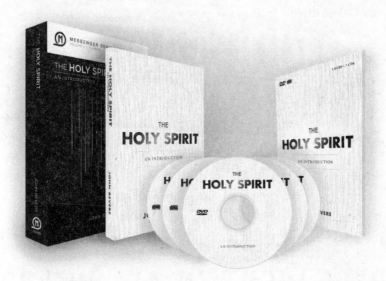

Learn about the Holy Spirit's personality and power—and how you can get to know Him better. With five teaching sessions and a special Q&A with John and Lisa Bevere, this curriculum will bring you closer to the eternal God who is passionately in love with you.

Included inside:

- 6 sessions on 2 DVDs and 3 CDs (30 minutes each)
- *The Holy Spirit: An Introduction* interactive book
- Promotional materials

Churches & Pastors

Local churches are the passion and heart of this ministry. Our Church Relations team connects with pastors, churches, and ministry leaders worldwide. It is our joy and honor to encourage leaders, pray for churches, provide life-transforming resources, and build authentic relationships. We'd love to connect with you!

USA: 800.648.1477   AUS: 1.300.650.577   UK: 0800.9808.933

 MSeries.tv

OUR FOCUS, OUR PASSION, OUR CAUSE

-JESUS-

PREEMINENT IN ALL WE DO.

TEACH: to instruct, edify, train, or demonstrate.

Messenger International always has been and always will be committed to the teaching of life-transforming truth. We are transformed through the power of God's Word, so it is our aim to further equip individuals, churches, and leaders through God-inspired teaching.

REACH: to touch, connect, stretch, or get a message to.

We have a dedicated global focus to make these messages available to pastors and leaders regardless of location or financial position. We support this work through the translation and distribution of our resources in over 60 languages and through our broadcast *The Messenger*, which reaches into over 150 nations.

RESCUE: to save, free, release, liberate, and restore.

The Church is His hands and feet to a lost and hurting world. Poverty and the tyranny of human trafficking have imprisoned multiplied millions. Messenger International is committed to rescue, restoration, and empowerment both near and far.

MESSENGERINTERNATIONAL.ORG